EARNING MY SPURS

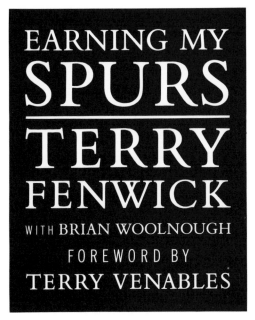

EARNING MY
SPURS
TERRY
FENWICK

WITH BRIAN WOOLNOUGH

FOREWORD BY
TERRY VENABLES

MAINSTREAM
PUBLISHING

First published in Great Britain in 1989 by
MAINSTREAM PUBLISHING COMPANY (EDINBURGH) LTD
7 Albany Street, Edinburgh EH1 3UG

British Library Cataloguing in Publication Data
Fenwick, Terry
 Earning my spurs.
 1. England. Association Football. Fenwick, Terry
 I. Title   II. Woolnough, Brian
 796.334′092′4

ISBN 1-85158-222-3

Typeset in 11½pt Imprint by Bookworm Typesetting Ltd., Edinburgh.
Printed in Great Britain by Billing and Sons Ltd., Worcester.

Dedicated to George and Nicholas, my greatest fans.

CONTENTS

Foreword by Terry Venables   9

CHAPTER ONE   *Life with Terry Venables*   13

CHAPTER TWO   *Big Mal, Venners and the Bald*   19
                   Eagle

CHAPTER THREE   *My England Regret*   31

CHAPTER FOUR   *The 1988-89 Season*   37

CHAPTER FIVE   *The Players*   161

FOREWORD

by Terry Venables

PLAYERS LIKE Terry Fenwick are vital to every side in football. I call them backbone players, men of character and determination who hate losing. They are winners.

That's why in December 1987 I had no hesitation in making Terry my first Tottenham signing. He cost Spurs £550,000 and, believe me, it was money well spent. I had been at White Hart Lane for a few weeks and soon realised that one of the players we needed was someone with Fenwick qualities. It is fantastic to have stars like Paul Gascoigne and Gary Lineker in your team but you have to have the Fenwicks too. Terry will not attract the public through the turnstiles or lift a game with a touch of genius but he is just as important to my future plans and team building projects at Tottenham.

I have known Terry a long time and have always admired his mature approach to the game. At Crystal Palace as a youngster he surprised me with his attitude – it was behaviour way beyond his years. He was able to cope with situations without getting upset or worried and that is rare in a teenager. You normally have to nurse kids along; give them a few games and then rest them before bringing them back again. Terry was different and he has maintained that mental toughness throughout his career.

At Palace in those early days Peter Nicholas was made of the same stuff. Graham Roberts, Spurs' former player who went to Glasgow Rangers and who is now skippering Chelsea, is another. They are men who have an inner drive and who give you one hundred percent regardless of situation or time. It doesn't matter if it is an FA Cup final or a League game that means nothing on a murky day in January, Fenwick will give you everything.

I like to think we could have another in Guy Butters. Guy came into the side last season and simply refused to be dislodged. I kept expecting to have to rest him, only to add him to the list of character players. It is not something you can teach a player. You are born with inner drive and determination – they are leadership qualities.

This is the second time I have signed Terry Fenwick. When I left Palace to go to Queen's Park I knew that if I could get him I would take Terry to Loftus Road, and was delighted and surprised to discover that Palace were willing to sell. It was the same when I came to Tottenham. I had kept tabs on English football while in Barcelona and knew that Fenwick's reputation had grown with club and country at Rangers. And I soon realised that Spurs needed someone like him.

He is a players' player. He is not going to split the opponents' defence with a 40-yard pass like Gazza, but he will always be there, at the heart of the matter. He is a player you can rely on and if there are any Tottenham fans who have doubted his ability they will, I'm sure, appreciate him before the new season is over. He is the kind of player you grow to appreciate without even noticing. His level of consistency in the 1988-89 season was high considering our disappointing start.

The fact that we recovered so well and finished sixth gave everybody tremendous satisfaction and encouragement for the future. I have never had any doubts that Spurs will soon be back right at the top where they belong, and we are building a side to challenge Champions Arsenal, Liverpool and all the other giants of football. It is the reason I returned to English football with Spurs, to win the big prizes.

It's impossible to say that my team building has been completed because clubs like Spurs are always in the market for top class players. That is why we went to Gary Lineker the moment we knew that he was available and realistically in

Terry Venables is delighted to have captured Terry Fenwick for Spurs.

our price bracket. We have some wonderfully gifted players at Spurs and I am sure the football we play will help put a smile back on the face of English football. But it can't always be showbiz-style and there are going to be days when you have to earn the right to play your attractive football.

That is why players like Terry Fenwick are vital. Spurs should be grateful to have him.

CHAPTER ONE

Life with Terry Venables

WHEN I left County Durham and the north-east as a 15-year-old schoolboy my parents warned me about London, especially the crafty Cockneys. 'You be careful and keep an eye on people like that,' my father told me as I began my career in football by signing for Crystal Palace. A few years later I met Terry Venables. He was just the kind of bloke my father had talked about. Crafty, confident, Cockney, funny . . . Terry was all of those rolled into one and I admit now that at the start I didn't know how to figure him out.

Thirteen years and three clubs later no man has been a bigger influence on my career than Venables. He is the best coach I have played under, has more fresh, stimulating ideas about football than any person I have been involved with, and at the start of the 1988-89 season we found ourselves together at the beginning of a real adventure. The task was to make Tottenham Hotspur Football Club, one of the big clubs in England, great again.

Venables had arrived as the great messiah in November 1987. He had parted company with Spanish club Barcelona and said 'yes' to Spurs, one of the clubs he played for in his career. And how Tottenham needed the master touch of the man regarded as one of the great managers in the world. They had been rocked by the sacking in disgrace of David Pleat and lost their way totally; the North London giants were in trouble and needed rebuilding.

I was Terry's first major signing and when I met him again after his three-year spell in Barcelona (where he won the Championship in his first season and took the Spaniards to the European Cup) he hadn't changed one bit. Just like my dad said, he was still bouncy, confident and, yes, a real crafty Cockney. It was as if he hadn't been away and I was talking to the same man who had influenced me at Palace and then signed me and developed my career at Queen's Park Rangers.

I was happy to sign for Spurs because, firstly, they were a big club and, secondly, I knew Terry Venables had the job of building a new era and I fancied being in at the start. Arsenal also wanted to sign me and I had spoken to their manager, George Graham. On paper Arsenal were the obvious choice because they had had two good seasons under Graham and the signs were that they were going from strength to strength. But I got the impression that I would have been only a squad player at Highbury, a signing of experience to help the development of Graham's young, impressive side. I would certainly have started at right-back, which is not my favourite position.

There was no choice to make after sitting down with Terry. He told me about his plans, the kind of player he wanted to sign, the football he sought from Spurs, and it was the challenge I was looking for.

I signed for £550,000 the next day.

My father, and I, for that matter, would not have believed it all those years ago when I arrived in London. I wouldn't have put money on playing for three different clubs for a man whom, at first, I didn't understand. But you learn

Early days at QPR.

I don't score very often, but every goal is worth celebrating. This one for QPR gave me a lot of pleasure.

quickly under Venables, on and off the field. If you are straight with him, he will be straight with you. He treats his players like adults. He demands respect and he wants the best for himself, his club and his players. At the start of the 1988-89 season he wanted nothing but the best for Tottenham Hotspur.

CHAPTER TWO

Big Mal, Venners and the Bald Eagle

THE REASON this devoted Sunderland supporter left the north-east was because of Malcolm Allison. Big Mal, as he is still affectionately known throughout football, decided to sign the outstanding 16 kids in the country for Crystal Palace and develop them into the best side in the land. We were to become known as the team of the Eighties.

I had been spotted playing for Seaham Schoolboys in a tournament in Jersey by Dennis Allen, the uncle of Clive, another kid in Allison's array of talent at Selhurst Park. I tore up my roots in the North-East because Allison impressed me with his knowledge of the game, his ideas and the way he went out of his way to make sure I didn't slip through his net. On one occasion he flew up to Durham with a Palace director just to watch me in a youth game.

Any boy would have been impressed with that and it was probably the thing that made up my mind for me. Palace were also getting a lot of publicity with an FA Cup run into the semi-final and Allison was centre stage, just as he has always been throughout his career.

Malcolm was fantastic with those kids he brought together in South London. There were players like Kenny Sansom, Peter Nicholas, Jerry Murphy, Vince Hilaire, Billy Gilbert and me all in the same team. Malcolm would spend more time with us than he did with the first team and he made sure the club was in good hands from top to bottom. He brought in coaches like John Cartwright, Terry Venables, Allan Harris and Arnie Warren, who was known as Mr Fix It on the London club circuit.

I realise now that Malcolm was five, probably ten years ahead of the time in his coaching and ideas. Before arriving at Palace we were so conventionally coached, staid in our ways, but he taught us a new dimension. Some of the things he asked us to do seemed wrong at the time and yet it didn't take long before the players realised that he was dead right. Terry was the same and he had the ability to simplify Malcolm's ideas. Terry would cut corners and eliminate a lot of the instructions that English players found difficult to master.

When Malcolm was eventually sacked in 1976 Terry was tailor-made to take over the reins. He was ready for it and the players were happy to work under him. The club had fallen into the Third Division by this time. I was still only a kid and yet I knew that Venables would get it right. It has been a feeling I have carried with me throughout my career.

Terry stamped his authority on the players with his coaching ability, knowledge and enthusiasm and none of us questioned whether he was right or wrong. The fact is that we enjoyed it and had great fun developing as a side and as individuals. Throughout my career I have never known anything else except coaching of the highest standard, coaching the Venables way.

I made my Palace debut as a 17-year-old in a 2-2 draw at White Hart Lane against Spurs and it was a match that just whetted my appetite for bigger things. I have always been determined and there is definitely a streak in me that drives me on in a bid to get to the very top.

As I expected, the young players at Palace were in good hands with Terry and the so-called team of the Eighties developed. It was not our name tag but one given to us by the media as we won promotion to the Second Division by beating Burnley 2-0 in front of a record crowd for Selhurst Park, 51,482. There must have been a further 10,000 people locked outside for a game that pulled at the nerve ends all night until we broke the deadlock. We had to win otherwise Sunderland would have pipped us, and I can remember looking around the dressing-room after the game and thinking that the songs and champagne corks drummed out the message that this time we could go far, if only it would stay together.

It was a big 'if' because Palace are and will always be a small club compared to the big boys of football. It was, and is, a pressure to live with when you have a manager like Terry Venables because he is always going to be looking for new horizons. And if he can't find them with you, he will go looking for them elsewhere.

Sure enough, in 1980 Terry quit the club, and although it shook football the players were not really surprised, even though it was a terrible blow for a group of kids who knew that they were capable of taking on anyone, anytime. I was flying back from an England Youth trip when I heard the news. Apparently the break with the club had been building up inside Venables for some months. Palace were selling some of their land off to food giants Sainsburys and Terry had told us that he had been promised some money to strengthen the team in the transfer market. It

21

never materialised and he had a running battle with the then chairman Ray Bloye. Venables' exit was the signal to break up the best young side in the country. They put Arnie Warren in charge and then even recalled Malcolm, but it was never the same.

Terry had walked out of Palace and taken over at Queen's Park Rangers. Before long I was happy to join him in a £250,000 deal that also took Mike Flanagan across London to Loftus Road. Some of the Palace directors were furious because Flanagan had only been signed from Charlton for £650,000 a few months earlier but Malcolm had agreed to the deal and, I understand, knew that Palace needed the money. It still seemed a giveaway to me, or a great piece of business by Terry.

I was happy to move and establish myself in a position that I favoured. All through my career I have been known as a utility player, and that is something I haven't encouraged. I am comfortable at full-back or midfield but my favourite position is at the centre of the defence, especially being used as the spare man in a sweeper system. I believe I read the game well and was grateful to Venables for playing me, eventually, as a central defender. He certainly signed me as one for Spurs although I did perform in midfield a few times towards the end of the 1987-88 season. But in the 1988-89 season I firmly established myself where I like playing most.

Terry hadn't changed when I arrived at Queen's Park Rangers, nor had his success rate. We won 12 out of 13 games and narrowly missed promotion to the First Division. He also went back to Palace for goalkeeper John Burridge.

Venables has always been full of ideas. He was the first man to introduce the 'hand signal' signs at corners, a tactic that is used by many teams today. At Palace if we put two hands in the air it meant a far post corner, one hand was a short rear post one. He is a perfectionist at free kicks. He says they should be more than just an advantage, they must be spot on!

At the start of the 1981-82 season, Queen's Park Rangers became the first club in the Football League to lay an artificial pitch, at their Loftus Road stadium. It was greeted with apprehension by the rest of the game and I have to say that the players didn't like it. The bounce was unpredictable, the run of the ball much quicker than a grass surface and players, especially tackling defenders, picked up grazes and cuts from the plastic. They said it would be a big advantage to us but we lost our first home game to Luton and never treated it like a home banker. None of the team relished the thought of playing at home and there were many other League grounds we preferred to our own.

The Venables magic worked again in May 1982, however, when he guided us to the FA Cup final as a Second Division side. We played Spurs and drew the first game with me heading a late equaliser, and then on the following Thursday we lost to a Glenn Hoddle penalty. But we played well enough in both matches to prove that another Venables team was emerging. We had good players in the side like John Gregory, a typical Venables signing who masterminded a lot of his ideas on the pitch. We were also unlucky that defender Glen Roeder missed the replay because of suspension and Clive Allen had to drop out with injury.

The following season we won promotion as Second Division Champions, ten points ahead of Wolves and 15 points in front of third-placed Leicester. From 10 October we were never out of the top three and it was another triumph for the man who was now regarded as one of the best managers in the game. The mighty Liverpool had won the First Division again and I fully expected Terry to strengthen the side and have a crack at beating the very best.

Amazingly, he only had one season in the First Division with us and we qualified for Europe. Then he quit Queen's Park Rangers in the summer of 1984 to take control of one of the big club sides in the world, Barcelona. I can't say that it was a total surprise, because a month before I had sat in his office and discussed continental football with him. He asked me then if I fancied playing in Spain. I laughed it off and didn't put any importance on the conversation. Then suddenly he was gone and I realised that he had already been thinking of Barcelona in those weeks before. Was it an offer to me? Who knows? I have never asked him. You can't look back. Life had to go on. We were approaching a season in the First Division and it was an important season for me.

Venables is certainly someone for a challenge. It doesn't have to be in football and he has done more in his life than most people achieve. He puts 'everything in' and there are not many people who can master so many different situations, mainly all at the same time! He is a great coach, has

My late equaliser against Spurs in the 1982 FA Cup final.

written books and television films and runs a string of busi-
nesses. I feel I know him better than most people, and yet
it wouldn't surprise me if he did something tomorrow that
stunned us all.

It was a farce when Venables left. Queen's Park Rangers
chairman Jim Gregory couldn't believe his favourite son
had gone and Gordon Jago, another former manager, was
brought back from America where he had been with Tampa
Bay Rowdies. Jago called all the players together and told
us what he wanted and expected. Twenty-four hours later
he was sacked with no real explanation to the staff.

Then Alan Mullery was appointed and I didn't think it
was going to work right from the start. Mullery was unlucky
because the ghost of Venables was still around the club and
whoever had taken over was going to experience problems
with the memory of a successful manager. But instead of
pulling us together as a unit he tried to change things,
especially the system which had brought so much success.
Mullery seemed a little in awe of Venables and tried to
blast the ghost away. What he should have done was let the
players continue with the same system and slowly tickle it
until he got us playing his way. We started that season well
enough but after only a few months, in December, he was
sacked by Mr Gregory. It was no surprise to the players, the
public or the media.

By that time I had signed a new four-year contract with
Rangers and it is probably one of the few decisions I have
made in football that I regret. I should have either waited
to see how the club developed or agreed a shorter contract.
It was interesting that when I first signed for Rangers, and
then Spurs, the contracts were negotiated by Terry but
when I discussed a new deal with QPR all the meetings
were with chairman Jim Gregory. I spent many pre-season
mornings at his home talking over the contract and couldn't
help feeling that I should have been discussing it with the
new manager. Jim Gregory had allowed Terry to run the

playing side of the club without any interference, and it seemed that he had resigned himself to the fact that the club would never be the same again.

Queen's Park Rangers eventually appointed Jim Smith, who had walked out on Oxford, as "Mullers" successor. Smith is known in football as the Bald Eagle and he soon stamped his enthusiasm and authority on the players. The side developed under him and in 1986 reached the Milk Cup final, only to be thoroughly beaten at Wembley 3-0 by Oxford, Smith's old club!

Smith is the kind of manager who needs a good coach to work alongside him, especially when he is dealing with international players and is up against the best clubs in the country. Jim Smith never did a better day's work than appoint Peter Shreeves as his right-hand man. Shreeves had been Keith Burkinshaw's assistant manager at Spurs and took over at White Hart Lane for two years before being sacked. With Rangers he was a bright, intelligent coach who quickly inspired the players with his knowledge and tactical awareness. I believe that Peter Shreeves was a turning-point for Queen's Park Rangers.

In his first match alongside Smith, the start of the 1987-88 season, we won 3-0 at West Ham and you could see the players grow in stature and confidence. We began playing a system that Venables would have admired, with me playing behind Paul Parker and Alan McDonald and two full-backs, Mark Dennis and Wayne Fereday, who were encouraged to push forward. I thought we were heading for a great season because teams found it so hard to score against us, although as the winter progressed I realised that we lacked real quality up front. We just couldn't score enough goals.

Terry had made me captain of Rangers and it is a job that I enjoy. I am a forceful, verbal player who is not afraid to say what he thinks on the pitch, to teammates and opponents. Venables didn't sign me for Spurs as captain but it is a job I want. Gary Mabbutt has the job at the time of writing this book but if anything changed I would want to be made skipper of Tottenham. It is a role I would relish and treat as a great honour.

As Rangers improved in that first season with Peter Shreeves at the club, Jim Smith and recently appointed chairman David Bulstrode put a lot of pressure on me to sign a new contract. Mine was coming up for discussion and there had been a lot of speculation about Arsenal and Spurs. It was a difficult time for me. Bulstrode was fantastic and he drew up the kind of contract that I knew would be difficult to match by any club in the country. I was close to signing it, only to hold back and give myself a little longer . . . just in case one of the big boys came in.

It was a good position because I knew that there was a superb new contract waiting at Loftus Road to sign. Then one day Jim Smith told me that Arsenal had made an offer and I knew that the ball was in my court. Did I stay and take the easy option of the devil I knew, or move on and gamble? Sheffield Wednesday were also interested and Jim tried to push me to the North, but that was never on because Wednesday for me are too much like Queen's Park Rangers, a 'nearly' club.

The turn of events was amazing once the ball started rolling . . . Arsenal manager George Graham spoke to Jim Smith, Smith rang Sheffield Wednesday, I spoke to Graham and then met him the following day. But, with my testimonial year coming up at Rangers, Arsenal could not match QPR's new contract offer. Two days later Spurs came in and I spoke to Terry Venables for the first time since he quit Queen's Park Rangers. Then George Graham came back with an improved offer but once I had spoken to Terry my mind was made up. I signed the next day and was happy to join him at the bottom of the ladder for the third time.

First there was the team of the Eighties at Palace, then he rebuilt Queen's Park Rangers and took us to promotion and the FA Cup final and now it is Spurs' turn, and the next chapter in our series, I'm sure, has years and years to run.

I signed in December 1987 and the last five months of the season were, frankly, a nightmare. In the end I couldn't wait for the season to end. I found it hard, coming from a club on top of the world and full of confidence to one on the slide, not playing well and with the crowd on their back. Don't get me wrong, I have never regretted the transfer but I realised straightaway that Terry had taken on one of the toughest jobs of his career.

One of the main problems was that some of the players didn't understand him, or how he wanted to perform. I watched him taking a back seat and assessing exactly the talent he had in front of him. Tottenham had always played good football and yet they had a reputation of not being organised as a unit. That was Terry's first major job.

In those early matches the organisation was nil. Players did their own thing on the pitch: when we had the ball it seemed that everyone wanted it, when the opposition got the ball everyone tried to get it back and everyone was trying to score. It was a shambles, a mess inside and out, and before Terry, the players had no figurehead to lean on. Terry's arrival came just in time because a big club was on the brink of collapse. There was no heart, no feeling and major surgery was needed.

At QPR all the lads had a laugh and a joke. That never happened at Spurs in those early days. I knew that there was only one way the club could go . . . and that had to be up. It was impossible not to improve the situation.

When the season ended I promised myself to get fitter than I have ever been before, and decided to keep active during the summer and to return to pre-season training two weeks before the rest of the players. I was no longer

Ball practice at QPR.

a member of the England squad and had nothing to do in the summer except prepare and wait for what I knew was going to be the biggest season of my life, one of the biggest in the history of Tottenham Hotspur Football Club. There was certainly no turning back.

CHAPTER THREE

My England Regret

DIEGO MARADONA, the world's greatest player, came running towards me like an express train. He had already beaten two or three England players and the Argentina skipper was en route for one of the most brilliant goals anyone has seen. I was the last line of defence. And I was struggling like hell to make a decision.

That moment, on a Sunday in the Aztec stadium in Mexico City, will go down as one of the biggest moments of my career, and I will remember it for all the wrong reasons.

I was injured. I had been struggling throughout the World Cup with an injury I hid from the media and the fans and probably camouflaged too much from England manager Bobby Robson and his staff. I had also been booked and I knew that if I brought him down, which I should have done, I would have been sent off and lost to the competition. So I only made a half-hearted tackle and Maradona swept past me and scored the goal that will be remembered for the rest of all our lives.

I admit now that I should have brought him down. It was a mistake and one I regret. I also know that I probably made a mistake playing in those 1986 World Cup finals in Mexico. But representing my own country in a World Cup meant so much to me that I played in pain – an awful lot of pain – and it probably affected my performances.

The World Cup will remain one of the highlights of my career but I didn't do myself justice because of the injury and I only have bitter memories of the finals. I played with a severe injury and I didn't realise just how bad it was until the competition got under way. The pain was in my groin, rather like the pain of a hernia, and I was told that I had torn abductor muscles. What I should have done was forget all about the World Cup and stayed at home to have an operation and clear the injury up. I foolishly put ambition first, the pride of representing my country at the highest level, and cracked on and played in pain. It was a mistake because I was not at my best and I did further damage to the injury.

The longer the competition went on, the more it affected me. I played against Portugal, Morocco, Poland and Argentina but it was painful to turn, even run. We had ten days' rest after the domestic season and the injury had settled down. I initially thought I was perfectly OK again but the hard training grounds in Colorado, where we prepared for Mexico, did more damage and I was sore by the time the competition started. I missed the game against Paraguay because of suspension (Alvin Martin of West Ham took my place) but Bobby Robson recalled me against Argentina in the quarter-final.

Had it been a league game at home I would not have

England v. Argentina, quarter-final of the 1986 World Cup.

played. I received pain-killing injections and didn't do much training between matches. Those precautions didn't stop the shooting pains every time I tackled or stretched for an interception.

The Argentina match, now I look back, was a nightmare. I can still see Maradona running towards me and, of course, it was a hell of a goal. But I still say that he should have been stopped long before he reached our penalty area. Before me there were four attempts and it has to be asked: were they good enough? But he wasn't stopped and I knew I was in trouble, with Butch and Gary Stevens miles away. It was me against him and I didn't tackle him properly.

His first goal, as we now all know, was hand ball and I chased the referee back to the halfway line. The rest of the lads seemed to be stunned but the Tunisian official, a man named Bennaceur, appeared certain that it was a good goal. He must have lived the nightmare of seeing the goal played back on television a million times and has probably suffered enough, just as England has.

The strange thing is that when I returned from Argentina I didn't have the operation straightaway. Doctors kept telling me that I would be OK and rest would cure the injury completely. I even missed the first 12 games of the season waiting for the injury, which still hadn't been properly diagnosed, to go away. Then I visited a specialist in Harley Street who took just ten minutes to recommend a hernia operation, and when he operated he discovered that my inside was a mess. I had played on so long that the hernia had bled back into the abductor and I had two nasty tears. I had left it so long I had completely lost the muscle and I wonder whether the plastic pitch at Queen's Park Rangers had anything to do with the deterioration.

This is the first time that I have mentioned my World Cup dilemma and I thought for a long time that maybe I had blown my England future. My international career has certainly gone backwards, especially after I took a lot of "stick" in the press about my performance in Mexico. It is crazy that I have only had two serious injuries in my career (the other was ankle ligament trouble) and that the second should come before the biggest competition any footballer can play in. Argentina was my 19th England cap and I worry that Bobby Robson holds my display – and my injury in Mexico – against me.

It was a relief therefore to be called up to the squad for a friendly in Israel in February 1988 as a late replacement. I even got on as a second-half substitute for Mark Wright and gained my 20th cap. I was surprised to be picked because I had played some good stuff for QPR all season and only got selected after joining Spurs and struggling along with the rest of the players. It just shows you that playing for one of the big clubs does influence people. It shouldn't, but it clearly does.

Pre-World Cup training in Colorado, USA.

All I can hope now is that I play well enough to break back into the England side. It is going to be tough because two years is a long time to be out. Terry Butcher is back after his broken leg and is a certainty to play; Tony Adams seems to be his first-choice partner and there will be others like Mark Wright, Dave Watson and Gary Pallister pushing hard. And two central defenders I believe will break through are Des Walker of Forest and Paul Parker, my old teammate at Rangers.

It is up to me and Spurs. If we do well right from the word go I will be pushing for a recall. If we struggle then I will probably have to wait a little longer. Yet, deep down, I don't believe I will play for my country again. One thing is sure, I don't want the memory of Diego Maradona as my last reminder of international football.

That still hurts more than the damn injury.

CHAPTER FOUR

THE 1988-89 SEASON

Welcome Gazza
All-change at Tottenham

WE REPORT back for training on 20 July and Terry is typically positive. He calls the players together and tells us to set our sights for the forthcoming season. That only means one thing – he wants the Championship. It is no idle threat from someone who clearly believes Spurs are good enough to be right at the top of the First Division. Only time will tell.

He has always been the same. At Palace and Queen's Park Rangers it was different players and new situations but the determination and confidence has been the same. Terry Venables doesn't like dealing in second best.

The first person I bump into is Paul Gascoigne, our new £2 million signing from Newcastle who has arrived at White Hart Lane on the back of some amazing publicity. He is

The amazing Gazza, the Clown Prince of White Hart Lane.

being acclaimed as the club's saviour and new Messiah and I only hope that he doesn't believe everything he reads about himself. It is going to be tough for Gazza, especially leaving the North-East for the first time and still feeling that his roots are back in Newcastle.

It is no surprise to see him because Terry told me at the end of last season that Gascoigne was going to be his number one target. He fancies him strongly and Paul is clearly going to be a cornerstone of our attacking ideas once the season gets under way.

I know exactly what Paul must be going through. I made the same journey south all those years ago and it is tremendously tempting to keep going home to see your family and friends. When I was at Palace I went back at every opportunity and the club usually allowed me to return every six weeks. The homesickness lasted about a year. This first season in London is going to be vital for Paul. He must establish himself in the team without feeling like a little boy lost and people shouldn't expect too much of him too soon.

I played against him twice last season and he is certainly not short of confidence for someone so young. He talks on the pitch all the time and carries that joking, carefree attitude into his private life. I believe the confidence thing is a great deal of 'front', however. It is really hiding a bit of insecurity, and if Paul is honest he would probably admit that he still needs his family around him. He does one or two things in training that suggest he is feeling the strain of living away from home and he once got fired up over a silly incident. I think the fact that he isn't married will help, as wives can spell aggravation if you are playing away from your roots and trying to make the grade in a different environment.

Our other big new signing is Paul Stewart, the Manchester City striker who has arrived at Spurs for a reported £1.7 million fee. The boss is spending a lot of money and clearly he feels the need to rebuild.

Stewart is new to me and I have only caught glimpses of

him on the television. It is a pity that he must miss the first four matches of the season through suspension and, like Gazza, he is going to need time to settle. I wouldn't expect much from him for the first month when he does start to play, but he looks strong and a handful once in full flow.

Stewart and Gascoigne make five new signings at Spurs, following the arrival of Paul Walsh, goalkeeper Bobby Mimms and me at the end of last season. It seems certain that there will be others because Spurs are being linked with everyone and anyone in the papers. I can't believe some of the names. Terry is good, though – he keeps the players informed.

There have also been a number of outgoings and it is certainly all-change at White Hart Lane. Clive Allen, Nico Claesen, Johnny Metgod, Tony Parks and Ossie Ardiles have all gone. Terry is no fool and must have weighed up what he wanted as he sat back and watched the team struggle towards the end of last season. It was important for some of the big names to go because there has to be a new era at Tottenham and you don't build a new future with old, established players who have become part of the furniture.

Ossie was the best example. He had to go because he had become a larger-than-life figure, an institution. It was important to break up the old Spurs and bring in the new, and Ossie and others had to go. Terry knows what he wants and he wanted some of the players out of White Hart Lane as quickly as possible. By the end of season 1987-88 Ossie was finding it hard to keep pace with the First Division and picking up injuries, but nothing should be said against him. He has been a marvellous figure in English football over the last ten years. Others such as Nico and Johnny Metgod were never first-team regulars under Venables. Terry sees things early, he would have made up his mind about these players soon after walking into the club.

We have started using the sweeper system in training, the same formation the boss sometimes made work at Palace and Rangers. But there are signs that it isn't going to be so successful and Terry is making moves to revert to a 4-4-2 formation. It is significant that all Terry's success has come by using the flat back-four. It is no good asking players to perform in a certain way if they are not ready or good enough to get it right, and I don't believe we have the full-backs at the club yet to make a success of the plan.

I like the sweeper system and over the years have had a lot of success playing that way. Most players enjoy it and, given the chance, would like to see most clubs in the First Division employing it. At Rangers under Terry I played behind the defence with full-backs Warren Neill and Ian Dawes being used like two wide midfield players. Jim Smith and Peter Shreeves reintroduced the system at the start of season 1987-88, with Alan McDonald and Paul Parker playing in front of me, with Wayne Fereday and Mark Dennis pushing up from full-back.

I have always been keen to keep fit all the year round and I combine my training and playing with games of squash and as many rounds of golf as I can fit in. I trained on my own for ten days before the other lads returned and then we had four days' heavy-duty endurance training at the club's training HQ in Mill Hill before flying to Sweden on Monday, 25 July.

It is a four-match tour spanning a week and Terry reminds us that we must take it very seriously. It is the start of the real Venables era and he wants all the players together to help build up the family atmosphere and camaraderie amongst the players.

Tuesday, 26 July. Nederslov Danningelanda 1 Spurs 4. (Walsh 3, Stewart)

The first game is always the easiest on tour because the programme is meant to get harder the longer you are away.

We got four but Paul Stewart still had a nightmare in front of goal. It was his debut for the club and he began to get uptight as at least six chances went begging. When he was brought down for a penalty he quickly picked himself up and scored. We hadn't discussed who the official penalty taker should be but we were all happy to see him get off the mark, even though it was a friendly.

I am not sure who will take the penalties when the season kicks off officially. I took them for Rangers and always feel confident. If I am asked I will say I want to take them.

Thursday, 28 July. Trelleborgs 0 Spurs 3 (Fenwick 2, Moran)

One of the positions to sort out will be centre-half. Chris Fairclough, skipper Gary Mabbutt and I all like to play at the centre of defence and three into two just doesn't go. I played at right-back in this game with Chris and Gary in the middle and I managed to get a couple of goals, the second a penalty.

It is halfway through the Swedish season and Trelleborgs are a good, strong side. They want to do well against us and it is a physical game with our goals only coming late on the match.

Sunday, 31 July. Gais 1 Spurs 1. (Walsh)

Tuesday, 2 August. Jonkopping 1 Spurs 1. (Waddle)

In between playing we have been training flat out. Terry really put us through it in an effort to build up our stamina and workrate and we looked jaded and worn out especially coming so soon after the 1-1 draw with Gais. Against this difficult team I missed a penalty, which is a replica of what happened in pre-season with Queen's Park Rangers a year ago. The defence played well, which isn't surprising because Terry has always made the defence his priority. We did miss a few chances but the signs are that we are getting it right.

Paul Gascoigne has shown some great touches on this tour and it looks as though he is going to bring a real touch of class to Tottenham, perhaps one day taking over from Glenn Hoddle.

But Gazza is going to have to live with the stirmongers and headline writers if he is going to survive. There are stories appearing back home that he has got to grips with a girl out here, which is a load of rubbish. But there is a girl who is pestering him and it seems she has been 'planted' in the hotel by a national newspaper from England and Gazza has been told to keep himself to himself by the club. There are rumours flying around and although Gazza is handling things well there are tell-tale signs that all this is getting to him. It is a shame but when you are high-profile, cost £2 million and play for one of the biggest clubs in the country, you are going to have to live with these kind of pressures. It's funny to see the lads hurry downstairs for breakfast every morning just to read the English papers for the next instalment of Gazza's lovelife!

We have packed an awful lot into ten days, players have been tried and systems changed. I think Terry will start the season using a 4-4-2 system although there are more warm-up matches to come.

Sunday, 7 August. Dundee United 1 Spurs 1. (Own goal)

Our toughest warm-up game so far. A good crowd created an atmosphere and the Jocks started to set about the old enemy. I played at centre-half and it was a tough match but one we enjoyed because we felt that it was a good test for us.

We used a 4-4-2 formation again and the boss seems to be coming down in favour of that. We are still not scoring enough goals for my liking and it is difficult because Paul Stewart will be suspended for the start of the season, and Terry is having to plan without him.

Tuesday, 9 August. Reading 2 Spurs 1. (Gascoigne)

I don't think there is such a thing as a friendly any more, and it may be a mistake for big clubs to play so many build-up matches against lesser teams. This was a fierce, competitive match and far from friendly. They wanted to win more than us, and that reflects my thoughts. The minnows treat games like this as a real challenge and a big match. Clubs like Spurs need to experiment and the edge isn't always there.

We didn't help ourselves, however, by playing poorly. Terry is disappointed, especially as it is our first pre-season defeat, but he tries to create good out of bad and takes us through the mistakes we made as a team. It is hard because he made a number of alterations before and during the match. I came off at half-time and there was a lot of chopping and changing.

I would say that, at this stage of the build-up, we are still two or even three weeks away from being a side ready to take on the First Division. The season starts on 27 August and this weekend we are involved in the international tournament at Wembley, playing against Arsenal, AC Milan and Bayern Munich, but we are not really ready for such opposition.

Saturday, 13 August. Arsenal 4 Spurs 0.

A nightmare from start to finish. I didn't think we were ready for such a tournament and the game, seen by a big Wembley crowd and millions more on television, only highlighted the work we still have to do. We are a new-look Spurs team trying to mould together and Arsenal, who have been playing under George Graham for two seasons, cut us to ribbons. I don't believe we should have agreed to enter the competition, and that is not sour grapes, just harsh reality.

The defeat is a hell of a shock to us and on the day nothing worked. Arsenal were fitter, more organised and at least three weeks ahead in preparation. I feel sorry for our fans having to swallow a defeat like this to our main rivals so close to the start of the season.

It is a pressure tournament and Arsenal are just polishing up where they left off. We are still rubbing down the bodywork.

Sunday, 14 August. AC Milan 2 Spurs 1. (Fenwick)

I feel as if we have played half a season in one weekend. This was not such an emotionally draining defeat but still a defeat, and one we could have done without. We are happy to get away from Wembley and I sympathise with Terry Venables when he admitted "Never again" after being asked if he would enter a similar competition.

Monday, 15 August. Chelsea 0 Spurs 0.

We are playing too many matches. We need time on the training pitch with the manager to sort out the problems and iron out team play and preparation. But we keep having to jump in at the deep end to try and sort things out in a game. I am not happy about it and, again, we look a poor side.

We need a recuperation period and the press attention we are receiving isn't helping. Terry, of course, is high-profile, he has spent a lot of money and the media are taking great delight as we struggle on. But we will show them, we will get it right and then it will be our turn to laugh.

We still looked the better side on the night and missed chances to win the game. Paul Stewart came on at half-time, even though he can't start the season, and I think the boss could well start with young Paul Moran in the side.

Sunday, 21 August. West Ham 2 Spurs 0.

We are not giving ourselves a chance. We are not being allowed to think things over and the more matches we play the worse it will become. We need time on the training pitch, time to ourselves.

Thankfully the boss is sending a reserve side to Peterborough tomorrow for our last build-up match. We lose that 2-1 and everyone right the way through the club has a lot of work to do, with the big kick-off just five days away.

We are also having to live with incredible newspaper attention. It has become something of a joke at training every morning because we are being linked with new signings all the time. It just adds to the pressure at the start of the season and I wish we could be left alone to concentrate on the job in hand. It is as if everyone outside White Hart Lane is waiting, even hoping, for us to fail.

I admit I am very apprehensive about the start of the season. We have had some up and down performances and the side isn't together as a unit yet. The supporters will be very expectant when we kick off against Coventry (our bogey side, I am told) at White Hart Lane on Saturday.

I feel OK myself and I am always an optimist and a confident person. My professional attitude tells me to get the season started, get stuck in and see how things go. I would rather start the matches proper and fight it out in the middle. If we have some problems let's discover what they are, we might be surprised and find that everything gells into place.

Deep down I hoped to be Tottenham's skipper this season. I enjoy captaincy and was the leader at Queen's Park Rangers before I left for Spurs. But nothing has been said to me and I am delighted to play under Gary Mabbutt. But one day I would want it.

Saturday, 27 August. The Big Kick-Off.

Terry has named a squad of fifteen for the opening game against Coventry at home. All eyes will be on Gazza and I believe that he is going to be a sensation when he settles down.

He can certainly take over from Glenn Hoddle as the new idol of White Hart Lane and I believe he is a better player than Glenn, certainly a better player for the English First Division. Paul Stewart, our other new expensive signing, is suspended and Terry has opted to play a four-four-two formation.

The first game of the season is always special. Players gear themselves up for it over the previous weeks and you go into the big kick-off full of enthusiasm and optimism. I am slightly apprehensive because we have been letting in silly goals but there is confidence in the club despite the pre-season results. We know we are good enough to do well.

I must get myself an answering machine for my telephone at home. On Friday night I was bombarded with calls for tickets. It never stops and while I don't mind for close friends, people I haven't heard of for months, even years, come on and expect tickets at the drop of a hat.

The phone rang again at 10.30 this morning and I thought it was someone else wanting tickets for our game with Coventry this afternoon. It wasn't, it was a good friend of mine calling to tell me that the game was off. I just laughed and told him not to be so stupid. But he insisted that it was off and had been postponed because White Hart Lane was full of builder's rubble and not safe enough for supporters.

Fifteen minutes later the club called and confirmed the bad news and told me to report instead to the training ground for a practice match. What a let-down, what a downer. Just when you are looking forward to getting the season under way you get a sickening piece of news like this. I haven't felt so gutted for weeks. Over the last two days we

Fen and Ben the Doberman. Fen's the one on the right.

have been preparing mentally for the game, and what for?
Nothing.

There was a mixed feeling of anger and frustration at the
training ground when we all met up. We are not involved
in the big kick-off and there is nothing we can do about
it, except train and get the frustration out of our bodies.
Everyone is in the dark and Terry looks mad. If he knew
something was up he is keeping his feelings from the players.

Coventry are understandably mad and we gather that
there is to be a Football League inquiry. You can't blame
either Coventry or the League for their reaction, and my
first thought was that the club was out of order. They
must have known the game was in danger because of the
rubble and they should have made a decision on Thursday. Someone has to take the responsibility and it must
come from the top. It is our mistake and we must pay the
price.

The rest of today is a nightmare. There is nothing
worse than being a professional footballer and not playing on a Saturday afternoon. I fiddled with the radio on
the way home trying to pick up results, goalscorers and
pieces of news. Liverpool and Arsenal have made ominous starts. Liverpool won 3-0 at Charlton and Arsenal
trounced Wimbledon 5-1 at Plough Lane. They are certain
to be strong again this season but I hope it is not another
runaway Championship for Liverpool. It would be good if
there were a lot of clubs involved, especially some smaller
ones to spice up the season.

Monday, 29 August.

The start of a new week and we must begin again building
up for our kick-off. At least it is at Newcastle and that is the
talking-point of the next few days with Gazza going back to

his home club and Chris Waddle playing against the club he left a couple of years ago.

There is speculation about Terry signing one of his old players from Barcelona and the papers say that he is in Spain chasing someone called Nayim. It could be true because he wasn't around today although none of us have heard of the player. I think I will go and watch my old club Crystal Palace take on Chelsea tomorrow night.

Thursday, 1 September.

I can't believe the news. David Bulstrode, my chairman at Queen's Park Rangers and one of the most popular men in football, has died of a heart attack. It is unbelievable because I only saw him at Selhurst Park on Tuesday and he looked so fit and well.

It is a tragedy for football too. David Bulstrode had ambitions to become one of the rulers of the game and there is no question that he would have got to the top. He was already tipped to become the new President of the Football League. In my dealings with him I can honestly say that I found him straight and honest and the contract that he and Jim Smith wanted me to sign at Rangers was a very good one. But he understood when I told him that I wanted the new challenge of one of the big clubs.

Friday, 2 September.

We flew up to Newcastle for tomorrow's game, our big kick-off. I enjoy going to the north-east and Gazza, Chris and I have our families together at the hotel for a chat and some drinks. It is a big day for Paul tomorrow, his Spurs debut against his old mates and in front of a packed St James Park crowd and his family. He definitely looks nervous.

Saturday, 3 September. Newcastle 2 Spurs 2. (Waddle, Fenwick)

I slept until 11 o'clock before going for a short walk to 'wake up'. We had our pre-match meal of tea and toast at 11.45 before eating lunch at one o'clock. Terry had a team talk after we had eaten, stressing the dangers and going over the set pieces. We have trained hard this week and are ready, at last, for our season to begin.

After 20 minutes I wish this match had been called off as well. Before we realised what happened we were 2-0 down and struggling to hold on. Both Newcastle goals had come from the same kind of move, a long ball over our back four. We stood looking at Bobby Mimms in goal and he just stared back at us. They were goals that made Terry mad during the half-time interval. He was fuming with the defence although he insisted that we could get back into the game, especially after the final 15 minutes of the first half which we had controlled.

Paul looked drained and emotionally tired after the first half. The goals were a slap in the face to him and to us and the crowd were not helping him. They attacked him throughout and every time he went close to the Newcastle fans they tossed Mars bars at him and called him 'fat boy'. But it is something he is going to have to learn to live with if he is to succeed.

Directly the second half started we got back into the game with a brilliant solo goal from Chris. It was just the lift we needed and it wasn't long before we were pounding their goal and looking the stronger side. Midway through the

I believe I have got the wrong reputation with referees. I am tough but fair and I prove that I hate being in second in the tackle in these four shots against Wimbledon at White Hart Lane. My opponent is Terry Gibson.

second half I equalised with a header after a short corner. David McCreery, the man marking me, failed to pick me up. The Newcastle roar was quiet now and we should have completed a great comeback when Paul Allen missed a good opportunity from close in.

I played in midfield against Newcastle. It is not my favourite position but I understand that the boss has got to experiment and take a look at everything before deciding on his best line-up and system. The only thing that blotted our comeback for me was a booking in the second half. I was wrong-footed and my opponent went down after a tackle. I pleaded my innocence with the referee, David Scott of Burnley, but he didn't want to know. He said I body-checked and the book was out immediately. The trouble with referees is that there is no consistency. One week a man will treat you like a kid, the next week another referee will call you by your Christian name and talk to you as the match is taking place.

It seems that I have got a reputation and there is nothing I can do about it. If I let it worry me it would destroy my game, but I often make a tackle fearing the worst. They see it is me and get out the book. The trouble is that most referees look for the wrong thing and book you when there are much worse offences taking place in front of their eyes. Some players get away with murder, tackling over the top, and there are one or two whom you know you are going to have to protect yourself from. The verbal abuse off the ball has definitely got worse and elbowing is a foul now common-place in football.

I can be nasty, most players can. But I never use it as part of my performance. In my younger days I was probably too aggressive and have learned to calm down with experience and age. I am still very committed and Terry made me skipper at Queen's Park Rangers because he knew I liked to voice my opinion. He said that if the team was not playing well I would make sure they got a rollicking. Even if my own game is below par I have never been afraid to voice an opinion out in the middle.

I don't believe I have got a short fuse although I can look after myself. Venners has always said to his players that it is good to have an aggressive edge but not to flaunt it. Keep it up your sleeve when it is needed most. I have always kept that advice at the back of my mind and in the last five seasons have not been over 21 disciplinary points. There have only been a couple of suspensions and I don't think that is bad for a defender.

I have only been sent off twice in my career. The first was in the early days at Rangers when Emlyn Hughes was putting together a very raw, tough bully-bully Rotherham side. Emlyn was always a cry baby and in this match, a very physical game in which three players were sent off and two carried off on a stretcher, Hughes proved that he was also a con artist. We went up for a high ball and he went down as if he had been shot. I couldn't believe it as he rolled over at least 12 times but the referee fell for it and I was sent off. Within minutes Hughes was running around again but he had done his job, he had got me out of the game. I am sure he was delighted.

The other time was at Charlton when I clashed with Robert Lee and the crowd went so crazy that the referee panicked and sent me off.

The game today has certainly become more physical. Teams are pushing up, matches seem to be played in smaller areas, and with tactics used like those of Wimbledon and Watford, there are sure to be more confrontations between big centre-forwards and defenders. The ball is slung in long from deep positions and it is just a question of the bravest winning. This is when the use of elbows is being exploited by some forwards.

I was once cautioned for celebrating a goal and it led to a disciplinary case at Football Association headquarters at Lancaster Gate that sickened me. I was reported by the referee for celebrating because he said I incited the fans at Newcastle and I was eventually charged with bringing the game into disrepute. It is a crazy charge because I was just happy at scoring a goal for Queen's Park Rangers in front of my family at Newcastle.

When I got to Lancaster Gate the referee and his two linesmen all said that I was climbing the fencing in front of the home fans. I couldn't believe it. I must have been ten yards inside the perimeter of the ground but the three officials had obviously sorted out their story before they arrived.

Midway through the hearing I just stood up and said that it was just a pack of barefaced lies and if we were not going to have the truth we might as well pack up and go home. 'Just give me the punishment because you have obviously made up your mind,' I said and walked out. Sure enough I was found guilty, fined £400 and banned for one match. It was a joke decision and backed up by an amazing incident as I left Lancaster Gate.

One of the commission, came up to me, patted me on the back and said: 'I'm sorry but we had to make an example of someone. We knew you were not guilty, or would not do anything like that.' Cheers, FA! How can I trust you again?

If you can't celebrate a goal what can you do? I am sure these people just want to take the enjoyment out of football. I scored the next week against Liverpool and kept my hands down by my side. What a stupid situation for football to get itself into when there are so many other things to clean up and get right. That hearing sickened me more than anything I can remember.

I suppose they call me tough because of my tackling and I took terrible stick from Brian Clough recently. He went on television and said that I ran 30 yards to commit a foul on Nigel Clough. It was a damaging remark and one that I found insulting and out of order. But the Football

Association did absolutely nothing. They found me guilty of bringing the game into disrepute for celebrating a goal and yet something like that went unpunished.

I thought about complaining but what is the point? The FA are scared stiff of Brian Clough. It seems he can do and say whatever he likes. There are rules for him and rules for the rest of us. The FA, however, should be big and brave enough to come down hard on Clough – he deserves it sometimes. We know he is a larger than life character but that doesn't give him freedom to condemn fellow professionals. He gets too big for his boots, thinks he is bigger than the game.

The mood in the dressing-room is totally different after our fightback at Newcastle. It is one of relief and excitement. Terry is happier but he still gives us a rollicking for the two Newcastle goals. He is right because we could and should have won the game. He also praises our spirit. At least we haven't lost and that is important at the start of a long, long race in the First Division.

Monday, 5 September.

Terry is trying to arrange a friendly game for Paul Stewart. He is short of match practice and Spurs obviously believe that a game in the middle of this week will keep him ticking over. But the Football Association are blocking the proposed game because he is under suspension. It is a crazy decision and I just don't see the point in banning a player from a friendly: it isn't any different than playing in a match between the first team and reserves at our training ground.

Tuesday, 6 September.

I have a feeling that Terry is going to change the defensive system against Arsenal on Saturday. He is obviously worried about the ease with which Newcastle scored their goals and it looks as though he could be moving towards re-introducing the sweeper system. That wouldn't surprise me because he used it so effectively at Rangers, with the two full-backs pushing up into forward positions. I enjoy playing at sweeper: it gives you more time and certainly makes it harder for teams to score against you.

Friday, 9 September.

Terry still isn't saying anything but the signs are that I will be playing sweeper tomorrow. He obviously doesn't want us to worry about the tactics because this is a big game for the club and our supporters, especially after the Wembley fiasco against Arsenal. And, of course, it is our first home game of the season.

The old enemy Arsenal. Here Paul Merson is held off by Paul Allen as I wait for a mistake.

Saturday, 10 September. Spurs 2 Arsenal 3. (Waddle, Gascoigne)

Sure enough, we are playing with a sweeper. Terry tells us at our pre-match tactic talk. He says that he has been toying with the idea all week and I am delighted. I believe it is the best system for us, certainly until we sort ourselves out at the back.

Arsenal are a good side – we found that out at Wembley in the pre-season tournament. They are very strong in midfield and have a good engine, a team of athletes who cover a lot of ground up and down the field. They have a good mixture of flair and are a team who like to wear their opponents down. They compete and fight for the right to play their football.

We knew what to expect and yet they still took the lead and eventually went 3-1 ahead. I was delighted with our attitude at this stage of the game and when Gazza scored I thought we would get right back into the match. We had two goals disallowed for offside that television clearly showed were OK. But we got some of our pride back and I don't think we are going to be a pushover for any side.

Arsenal are clearly going to be one of the strong sides of the season. They have bedded down together over a couple of years although I am not convinced about their strike force. I believe they could come unstuck in front when the heat and pressure is really on.

Alan Smith is a good average striker but nothing special. He doesn't knock you about like Mick Harford at Luton and is not a natural goalscorer He is one of those players who is pretty good at everything and not top-class at anything.

Their strength is their organisation and the system that has been drilled into them. I can't see them conceding any goals. As for the Championship? I wouldn't put money on them yet.

My wife Amanda doesn't come to many of the games and we are still getting to know all the Spurs wives. Tonight we went out for a meal to drown my sorrows. I am not too despondent but, already, I don't like losing to our North London rivals.

Monday, 12 September.

Paul McGrath, Manchester United's central defender, is the latest player to be linked with us and reports say that he is meeting the boss in London sometime today. I know Terry still has two or three players in mind but the speculation surrounding new signings is very unsettling. At least McGrath is top quality and when he is fit and playing well there is no one better.

The fee is said to be £1 million and that is a little surprising because it seems a lot of money for someone who has a bad injury record, and who might just 'fall down' tomorrow.

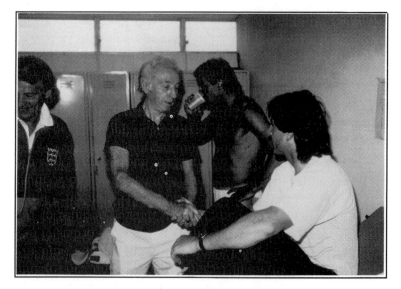

Fen meets the great Sir Stanley Matthews. Bobby Robson looks sideways while Peter Shilton satisfies his thirst.

I am sure that, if it came to an agreement, Terry would insist on a payment down and the rest to follow once McGrath had made a certain number of appearances.

We certainly need a big guy at the back and, deep down, I know that Terry would rather play a 4-4-2 system than the sweeper style we are adopting at the moment. We are playing the sweeper system because it suits the type of players we have, rather than the players he wants.

This is international week and Chris and Gazza are away on duty. It is not as lonely here as other clubs because, apart from Chris Hughton, all the lads are English.

I loved playing for England and I would jump at the chance of getting back in. But I have made up my mind that my England career is over. It should be, too, because it is high time some fresh, young new faces were introduced. Players like Paul Gascoigne should be in the England team now and it will be criminal if he is not picked against Denmark on Wednesday. Clubs don't pay out £2 million for things that players might do, they invest in quality and that is what Gazza is. It takes so long to break into the England side and I, like a lot of other people, am disappointed that the manager has kept such faith in his tried and trusted after the European Championships.

Had I been the England manager I would have taken eight senior professionals to West Germany and packed the rest of the squad with young players, kids really bursting to break through and make an impact. We need new blood in the side. Look at the Italians – they swept clean, went to the Europeans with a new-look side and reached the semi-finals. That boldness will probably guarantee them one of the best sides in the 1990 World Cup in their own country.

If Bobby Robson isn't careful we are going to be in the same position for the World Cup – if we qualify – as we were for the Europeans. It is crazy. There should be changes all along the line with players like David Rocastle, Gazza and Paul Parker bedded down in the side, not used for one or two matches and then discarded. But told that they have got a string of games to get used to international football.

The other thing that amazes me is our insistence that we can't play the sweeper system when every other country is good at it. The manager keeps saying that we can't do it because we don't play it at club level and players can't adapt. Bullshit. The players are good enough – or is he saying that we are not good enough to play the way he wants?

I know that players who look top-class in League football don't necessarily have to be international standard yet they have got to be given the chance. I would love to see Franz Carr of Forest given a try and how Nigel Clough hasn't been given an extended opportunity is beyond me. We know he doesn't have the pace of the really great strikers in Europe but he can be used in different ways and surely you can't make up your mind about him without looking at him first-hand?

The fact is that England has received a smack in the face after the European Championships. We didn't win a game and looked second-rate. If Robson had reacted by making changes at least we could have seen that something was trying to be achieved.

I am arguing for a new-look England against my own interest. If new faces are called up players like me will be discarded for good. But I have got 20 caps and am chuffed to have played that many times for my country. Yet, realistically and professionally, I know it is time to change. For the good of the country Bobby Robson has got to forget, and look forward.

Wednesday, 14 September.

Robson hasn't picked Gazza and has gone back to Steve Hodge of Forest. Hodge didn't even make the European Championship squad and this is the kind of selection that emphasises my point.

I didn't go to Wembley but we beat Denmark 1-0. It wasn't a good game. England played as though we were suffering a terrible European Championship hangover and I fear for the development of the team.

Friday, 16 September.

The facilities on Spurs' luxury coach are second to none. It's a real first-class hotel on wheels. After training we travel up to Liverpool and there is a full restaurant choice menu for lunch, all prepared by our own chef and cooked as we move up the M1. There are televisions, stereos, music systems, toilets and even a physio department for John Sheridan on board. The club leave nothing to chance for the well-being of the players.

We arrive in Liverpool early in the evening and after dinner at seven-thirty the players usually lounge around, watch television and have an early night. I am sharing with Walshy, two signings who arrived at the club at about the same time.

Queen's Park Rangers always played well at Anfield and my attitude against Liverpool is that if you see out the battle you have got a chance. Peter Beardsley has been causing team trouble by sitting in the 'hole' just behind the main strikers and we have decided to pull Paul Allen back in an effort to snuff out that problem.

Saturday, 17 September. Liverpool 1 Spurs 1. (Fenwick)

We played well and started superbly. Gazza stroked the ball around as if he was playing in his own back garden and Chris and Walshy missed early chances. They were good ones and would have given us the perfect start and a terrific boost at

Promoting the club's image is an important part of the job. Fen presents two youngsters with their trophies.

between the 18-yard boxes. It doesn't sound very much but when you have done half a dozen of box-to-box sprints you know whether you are fit or not. Then it is back to a game. I enjoy training but I'm not sure about these pitch-length doggies. The fittest player at the club would be between Paul Walsh and Chris Fairclough.

Gazza is a good trainer, which is encouraging to see because so often the really gifted players are not interested in doing hard work away from the games. They just want the ball all the time but Paul is prepared to get his head down and do everything. He is laughing and joking all the time as usual, and not shirking a thing.

We are normally given Wednesday off and Friday is a session for winding down and concentrating on the opposition. A short warm-up, a game of five-a-side and some set pieces. Then the boss will take us through the opposition, their strengths and weaknesses and tomorrow it is Middlesbrough at home.

Saturday, 24 September. Spurs 3 Middlesbrough 2. (Waddle, Fenwick [pen], Howells)

I normally keep to the same routine on home match days. You have to report to the ground by one-thirty for a players' meeting at two and some of the boys go in really early and eat at the restaurant. That is OK as long as you have completed your meal by 12.15, the deadline set by the boss. I normally stay in bed until about ten, then have a cup of tea and take the dog out for a walk to get my mind right. I don't normally eat anything before a game and leave home about midday for the journey into White Hart Lane.

On Friday and Saturday things have to be just right for me at home and I get touchy if the routine changes. I want to eat the right things and relax, and I certainly don't want any visitors in the house. It is easier when it is a midweek game because the kids are at school and friends are at work, but having a house full on a Friday before a game is not on. My wife Amanda used to find it a hassle but she has got used to it now.

We should get our first win of the season today and it is a real slap in the face when we start to struggle. We are a different team to the one who played so confidently against Liverpool and 'Boro go 2-1 ahead. None of us can believe it and the game only changes when Terry makes two substitutions in the last 15 minutes. On come David Howells and Paul Moran and we are a different side.

Suddenly we start to click, the workrate quickens and 'Boro start to panic at the back. I think to myself, 'Had we played like this throughout we would have won 10-0.' We equalise and then in the last seconds get a penalty and it is down to me to secure that first win.

I have always taken penalties and my attitude is not to worry about them. If they are in the first minute or the last you can only do your best. As I am walking towards the penalty spot I make up my mind which way I am going to strike the ball, and if the 'keeper guesses right that is all down to the rub of the green. I never change my mind and am certainly not one to study goalkeepers to see which way they dive. This time I guess right and we win, thank goodness. The sigh of relief can be heard all the way around the ground.

In the dressing-room someone says that our winner came in the fourth minute of injury time. But the players never really know how much time there is left and certainly in those last 15 minutes the time just seemed to shoot by.

The boss is happy even though we haven't played particularly well. 'Boro can argue that they were unlucky and yet these things even themselves out during a season. I am sure we are going to play well and lose before the winter is over.

Monday, 26 September.

It is the Littlewoods Cup tomorrow and we have been drawn against Notts County in a two-leg tie. We are away from home first and should get through without too much danger. I don't mind two-leg cup ties, especially when you are away from home first. We should be good enough to get a result and then kill them off at home.

I fancy us to do well in one of the Cup competitions.

Tuesday, 27 September. Notts County 1 Spurs 1. (Samways)

We started like we did against Liverpool and yet failed again to take our chances. The game should have been over long before we allowed County back into it with a goal. It came from another set piece which is worrying for us.

Vinny Samways equalised and we never looked in real danger although County did put us under pressure in the closing stages. It is a result that I would have predicted but no one is happy with the performance and we are still a long way off from getting it right. We will certainly have to improve against Manchester United at home on Saturday.

Friday, 30 September.

Paul McGrath is not joining us, which is no great surprise because the speculation has been going on for too long. A player doesn't usually sign if he can't make up his mind quickly, especially when the club buying is one of the biggest in country. The players are glad that the speculation is over.

Paul Stewart is free of suspension at last although he is only substitute tomorrow. The boss feels that after our recent results he needn't change the team.

*Saturday, 1 October. Spurs 2 Manchester United 2.
(Walsh, Waddle)*

They say history doesn't repeat itself, and we had a chance
to prove that wrong in the last minutes when, after coming
back from 2-1 down to make it 2-2, we were awarded a
penalty. I strode forward to take it and produce the same
result we had collected against Middlesbrough seven days
earlier. But Paul Stewart, who had come on as substitute,
came charging forward and demanded the ball. He had been
on fire since he came on and it was as if he had been waiting
all his life for the chance to play for Spurs.

He had been full of confidence and was so adamant that he
wanted to take it that I let him have the ball. I said, 'Are you
sure?', and he said 'Yes,' and I didn't think there was any
danger of him missing. When someone is that confident you
let them get on with it. He appeared more confident than
me and was no stranger to penalties. He had taken them for
Manchester City last season and converted one in pre-season
for us.

So up he charged and, unlike me, tried to break the net.
But the ball smashed against the underside of the bar and as
it came down I just failed to scramble it over the line!

It was a bitterly disappointing moment for us because
victory over United would have lifted the whole club.
Stewart was confident and wanted to take it and, as I
have said before, the line between missing and scoring is
fine. But I do feel that you should hit the target. I said
afterwards that I would be taking all future penalties, and
I meant it.

In the dressing-room Terry asked me what happened and
I explained that Paul was so confident I let him have it.
Nothing much was said. Paul didn't give any excuses and
the inquest was left until Monday.

We had taken the lead only for Mark Hughes to equalise
with a great volley and then they took the lead. Gordon

Strachan did well for them and Peter Davenport, wide on the left, caused us too many problems for comfort. United surprisingly took him off and that allowed us back into the game.

We had the chance to beat them and blew it, and that is a shame because there is still a buzz about United and to play against them will always mean something special. Paul Stewart will certainly never forget his Spurs debut against them.

Monday, 3 October.

Paul took some 'stick' today over his penalty miss although Terry is more upset about the Mark Hughes goal. It should have been avoided, he claims, and runs through yet again how we are being caught at set pieces.

Fen and big Frank – before I knocked him out.

There is speculation starting to rage in the papers about Bobby Mimms and the goals we are conceding. That won't worry Terry too much because he has always thrashed things out with the players inside locked rooms. If anything goes in the press from him the players normally know about it first, and that is good management. We are worried that a lot of goals we are conceding are coming from set pieces. We are so inconsistent because we will go long periods when we look watertight and then give a silly goal away from a corner or free kick.

At this moment Terry is talking to the defence as a unit rather than to Bobby on his own. He is stressing the importance of concentration and how most of the goals we have conceded this season could have been avoided. We also thrash out the problem that Davenport caused and discuss the fact that for too long on Saturday we looked lop-sided down the right-hand side. They are problems we must solve this week.

Saturday, 8 October. Charlton 2 Spurs 2. (Fenwick [pen], Allen)

Another crazy goal costs us victory. We had just fought our way back when the ball was switched back to Bobby. We were under pressure and it was the opportunity for him to hold on to the ball and then clear and allow us to re-organise. But he chose to throw it out to Gazza, who lost possession and Andy Jones chipped a great goal from wide of the box. It seems that every goal we concede needs an inquest. Gazza takes the blame but Bobby was at fault for throwing the ball out when we needed a bigger clearance. It is the same old story, we are creating our own downfall.

We had been in control of the game when they took the lead with a long shot from Andy Peake that deflected in off Gary Mabbutt and we had to come back the hard way again. I equalised with a penalty and Paul Allen made it 2-2 but this, again, was not a convincing performance. We are capable of so much more and the boss must be getting frustrated. I know the fans are.

Monday, 10 October.

Gazza has been picked by England again and he is chuffed to say the least. To me, however, he looks a little apprehensive and it wouldn't surprise me if all his super-confidence hides a few private nerves.

Tuesday, 11 October. Spurs 2 Notts County 1. (Fenwick [pen], Gascoigne)

Gazza was certainly confident tonight. He won us the game and put Spurs into the next round with a superb free kick from the edge of the area. We have seen him do it so often in training. The goalkeeper is still organising his wall when Gazza whips the ball into the opposite corner. He is so accurate and takes the goalkeeper by surprise. It is just another example of his great talent. It was decided in pre-season that Gazza would take most of the free kicks in danger areas. He was the big new signing and wanted to be involved with everything, and who can argue when he can pick out teammates from every angle?

Paul Stewart has still not scored and it is beginning to get him down. He is playing quite well but obviously needs a goal. Paul Walsh is the same and his situation is more critical. He is looked upon as a recognised striker and yet his scoring record is poor. It is upsetting for him because he

Earlier days with the England cricket team.
Back row left to right: *Viv Anderson, Gary Lineker, Gary Bailey, Dave Watson, Chris Woods and Mark Hateley.* Front row: *John Barnes, Terry Butcher, Glenn Hoddle, Fen and Chris Waddle.*

isn't doing it for the team and we need his goals, especially with Stewart still settling in.

There is no game on Saturday because England manager Bobby Robson has been given more time with his players to prepare for next Wednesday's World Cup qualifying tie with Sweden. It always seems strange when there is no game at the weekend. I hate postponements and this feels like the opening day of the season when the Coventry game was called off.

Terry had us in to play a full-scale practice match against the reserves and it is a good idea because it gets the 'Saturday' feeling out of your system.

This time, I suppose, a Saturday off has not come at a bad time. We are not playing well and we are under a certain amount of pressure from supporters and the media who, rightly, expect Spurs to get good results. On this

Cricket captain Fen parades his team sheet.

Saturday we don't have to do anything to satisfy anyone else.

Blank Saturdays for England's preparation are a good idea as long as the time is used properly but, knowing Bobby Robson, I doubt that it is.

I get mad when I keep hearing that the England manager doesn't have enough time with his players, or that we haven't got good enough individuals to blend into a team to take on the rest of the world. When I have been involved with the international set-up, there has been a hell of a lot of time wasted. They scream blue murder that they want the Football League to postpone matches and then when they get the players they waste the time.

The normal system when you report with England is to train in the morning and rest in the afternoon. But the training, I found, lacked inspiration and new ideas. You arrive keyed up and bursting to express yourself and it is a good feeling when you meet up with the squad, the best players in English football. But there is nothing to bring the best out of you and it is just a question of self-motivation. Of course you don't need inspiring to play for your country, but you need new ideas, fresh challenges, interesting new tactics. I searched for it under Bobby Robson but couldn't find it.

Bobby Robson, of course, is doing what he thinks is best for his team and the country. No one is blaming him for that and this is not a personal attack. I would be saying these things whoever was in control. Anyone who knows me will realise that I only criticise when I really believe something. It's just that I care passionately about England.

The one thing that amazed me was the fact that although we met up on a Sunday evening, it was Tuesday lunchtime before he announced the side and that left just one session, the following morning, for the actual team to play confidently together. Why wait? It is like blindfolding the players and playing a guessing game with the nation. There is so much time wasted while players train in groups and wait for the announcement.

I believe that Bobby just played a waiting game with the press and forgot about the players' feelings. If the squad is fit when they report on Sunday he must know the team he wants to play three days later. Surely no one is going to do so brilliantly in training to change his mind?

The afternoons are also a joke. Players just wander around the hotel trying to fill in the hours and beat the boredom. Why not have some set piece sessions in the afternoon, watch videos of the opposition, bring in other experts to discuss every aspect of being a professional footballer? I am sorry, but I don't believe that Bobby Robson comes over at all well. There is nothing new in his coaching, the players are not stimulated or surprised at anything they do with England. And that is wrong because when you are called the best you should have that something extra to produce peak performances. Don Howe is Bobby's right-hand man but, let's face it, his ideas on football are boring.

The big question mark aimed at England is why can't we get the best out of our players, why don't they perform for their country as they do for their clubs? If the truth was told, it is because the coaching is poor. You only have to look at our results over the last few years. We have achieved nothing. There is no imagination and we are stuck in a rut, way behind the rest of the world. I am very disillusioned and disappointed with the England set-up. When I was involved I often used to think to myself: 'There has got to be more than this, we are supposed to be the top of the tree.' But it never happened.

The trouble with Bobby is that he likes to keep so many people happy. He is too nice, and his biggest mistake is his handling of the press. He always gives them too much time, and even when they turned on him he didn't even wave two fingers and say, 'Stuff you'. That's what he should have done, and he would have gained more respect from

Terry Venables would make a good England manager.

the players. When I was playing they didn't have enough confidence in him and today he looks a worried man.

England just never look like winning a football match, especially when it matters. We should pick the best players for the job in hand, not stay with the tried and trusted all the time. Look at the opposition and choose accordingly, but it is always the same players and same tactics with England. The other countries change and we stay on the same line.

Take John Barnes, he never looks the same player in an England shirt and you must draw your own conclusions. Ask yourself why he never gets in the same positions as he does for Liverpool. He is simply not told to do what he is good at.

Take Glenn Hoddle, there is no one in Europe with more skill and yet we never got the best out of him. Never. He was asked to play on the right of midfield and that is a joke. If it is between Trevor Steven and Glenn for that position then you must go with Steven, but why even consider Hoddle there when his best position is in the centre of midfield? He should have been given a free role years ago, and should still be in the side today. Poor Glenn has been strangled by the system and bad management.

OK, I am biased, but Terry Venables would make a good England manager. Bobby Robson has been around for seven years and we have won nothing. How long do they want to give him? What makes a good England manager? Robson did a good job at Ipswich and won the FA Cup and UEFA Cup and was given his chance as manager of England, but you must be an outstanding coach before anything else.

When Terry went to Barcelona he got rid of the world's best player, Diego Maradona, after a couple of weeks and no one could believe it. But he saw what he wanted, the players he needed to play his way, and he went on to win the Spanish League and got Barcelona to the European Cup. People still say that he hasn't proved himself as club manager or coach in England. What do you have to do to prove yourself! Win things? In that case you might as well hand the job to Kenny Dalglish. No, for England, you have to be aware of styles, systems, tactics that every team in the world is using, and be ahead of the game.

I am disappointed with Bobby Robson, after working with him and now from the outside. I expect a better standard from the England manager. The Football Association have got to take some responsibility, otherwise we are going to struggle behind the rest for years. There are a lot of progressive, young brains desperate to express themselves and allow the development of the game, but they are being held back by stubborn, selfish people who won't allow the times to change. They are harming football for their own satisfaction. In America someone who isn't doing a good job, moves over and gives someone else a try. It is a good system. In England, however, we just say, don't worry, it will be alright next year.

When I was playing for England we used to have team meetings and I enjoyed voicing my opinions. Bobby and Don would listen to me and then just say: 'Right, let's move on.' It was as if they didn't want to listen. It went in one ear and out the other.

I hope Bobby and Don prove me wrong, I really do. I am not a person to criticise for the sake of it and repeat that this is not a personal thing. I want England to win as much as they do.

Monday, 17 October.

The Football League today deducted two points from our First Division total for the 'first day' postponement of the Coventry match. I think it is totally out of order and just couldn't believe it when I heard the verdict.

Terry went to the hearing with chairman Irving Scholar and Allan Harris took training. We knew the hearing was on but didn't worry too much about it because the matter was between the chairman and the club, and the builders.

To deduct the points is punishing the players for something out of our control. Are they now going to ask us for the bonuses we won while winning the two points? It is a joke decision, one that has angered the players, and a decision that pushes us towards the foot of the First Division. Things are going from bad to worse.

Tuesday, 18 October.

The attitude among the players today is one of anger, frustration and 'let's show them'. It feels as if everyone is against us and there is no doubt that a lot of people are taking great delight in seeing Spurs fail. The size of the club is such that it triggers off jealousy and there are a lot of people around who shake your hand when you know they would love to stick a knife in your back.

We held a players' meeting and decided to crack on together. In a way the verdict probably brought the squad closer. There is a real determination running throughout the club now.

Terry is just as disappointed as us and he said that he thought the decision by the League committee had been reached long before he and the chairman gave evidence, or the facts had been examined. 'They'd made up their minds,' Terry told us, and said that he asked the committee what was the point of Spurs travelling to Birmingham if they had already made up their minds. I would like to know what happens if those two points cost us the Championship, or push us into the Second Division after a relegation fight. I hope those men know what they were doing.

Wednesday, 19 October.

I didn't go to Wembley to watch England's World Cup goalless draw with Sweden, it was bad enough viewing on television. We should be beating teams like Sweden, especially at home, and there can be no excuses. It was a farce at the end with Gazza getting on for a few minutes. It was if the manager was saying, 'Here he is, I don't really want to play him but you said I need to give him a go.' What chance do you have to make an impact right at the end of a game?

81

Saturday, 22 October. Norwich 3 Spurs 1. (Fairclough)

More bad goals conceded and it is beginning to damage the morale of the side. There is some finger-pointing at each other, accusations. That is a sure sign that things are going wrong. The goals we gave away were pathetic and you would think that after working so hard on set pieces, all the players would be on their toes. But no, the concentration went again and we got punished.

Bobby should have done better with a free header but you can't only blame the goalkeeper. There is some bad marking going on. We are all in this together. After the points deducted blow this is a bad result for us, a real slap in the face. And a defeat that pushes us towards the bottom of the First Division.

The annoying aspect of the season so far is that no team has really outplayed us. I haven't been particularly impressed with anyone, except perhaps Middlesbrough who played some good football against us. The others have just taken the points from us, courtesy of our sloppy defending. But we are also not creating enough, or looking dangerous in the box.

Norwich are the team of the moment, one of the surprise sides in an upside down First Division, and yet I am not that impressed with them. They are sitting proudly on top of the First Division but they won't win the Championship. Their home form will let them down.

Sunday, 23 October

Terry has now been in charge for exactly one year, as the media are quick to point out this morning. They say we have won only seven times in the First Division in that time and there is no one more gutted about that than the manager. It is a diabolical record and he is getting a lot of stick over it but the players must take more responsibility. Terry is entitled to have expected more from us. We have let him down and between us Spurs have made a hash of it over the last year.

Terry has spent so much time with us, coaching and leading, and yet when we go on to the park we just seem to forget the basics. Seventy per cent of the goals we have conceded in his first year have come from set pieces, and that is diabolical.

We all accept the criticism and it is up to us to get ourselves out of trouble, up the table and into our true position in the First Division.

Tuesday, 25 October. Spurs 1 Southampton 2. (Own goal)

I still can't believe we lost this game. How did it happen? It is, I am afraid, the story of our season so far. We are the better side and yet lose. It is as if someone 'up there' doesn't like Tottenham.

You had to be at White Hart Lane to believe the result. We murdered them for football, scored an early goal and played like champions. The confidence was returning to the side and it felt right, it felt good again. Then, suddenly, they were back in the game thanks to a great volley from Glenn Cockerill, their midfield player who had been in the news recently after having his jaw broken by a 'left hook' from Arsenal's Paul Davis. Cockerill hadn't finished with us, however, and scored a winning goal. I just sat in the dressing-room looking into space and wondering what on earth we had to do to get the lucky break we need.

Terry is tearing his hair out, and, again, we have conceded a goal from a corner. Cockerill's first, although it was a fine shot, was a goal that should have been avoided and would have been had Gazza remembered the player he should have been marking. He was supposed to be standing on exactly the spot from which Cockerill struck his shot. Terry pleads with him: 'Where were you, Gazza?' But it is too late, the damage is done and all Paul can say is sorry.

Wednesday, 26 October.

Newcastle beat Middlesbrough to send us to the bottom of the First Division. It is rock bottom for Tottenham and a terrible blow to the morale of the club. We have the players, we have the ability, why are we struggling? I still have faith in us to pull clear – things, after all, can only improve.

Thursday, 27 October.

Terry called us all together for a players' meeting. It was a clear-the-air talk-in and he stressed that it was no good feeling sorry for ourselves, we are in this together and it is up to us, all of us, to get out of the mess.

He urged us to improve our concentration, particularly at the back, especially from set pieces, and stressed that it was no good knowing that you are the better side if you keep losing the matches. He is a good motivator and the atmosphere was soon cleared. We went into that meeting feeling down and worried and left believing we could take on the world.

That is good man-management and the boss deserves credit because he is under tremendous pressure from the media. He has his critics and they are out to rubbish him. But Terry can take it and I know that one day, I hope soon, he will have the last laugh.

The latest anti-Tottenham game from the critics is a series of Spurs jokes, especially from the tabloids. You know the kind of thing: what is the difference between the Star of David and Spurs – the Star of David has got six points! Great fun so long as you don't play for or support Spurs, although the players are taking it well. Before training we always pick up the papers and have a chuckle at the latest jibes, although deep down I know there is a strong feeling that we want to 'stuff it' to these people.

The jokes are coming thick and fast because of the size of the club and that is fair enough. What amazes me is that Terry's critics are now saying that they expected so much more of him, yet on the other hand they say that he has not proved himself to be considered as the England manager!

There is certainly no change in the boss. He rides these situations well and even joins in the jokes. He walked past a group of players reading the papers this morning and shouted: 'Everything OK? You don't mind if I just go upstairs and hang myself!'

It is vital that we keep the spirit going. Terry has also called us together to push home how important it is to stand up for one another. He warns us that there will be attempts to split the camp and situations will occur to get in between us. He says never criticise one another in public and stay loyal to the club and yourselves. 'This will pass, we will get it right' – and he is talking sense.

It would be easy, for instance, to have a go at Bobby Mimms. He is having a bad time and we are conceding silly goals but what good would it do the team, and Bobby's confidence? We all know that we are not playing well as a team.

Saturday, 29 October. Aston Villa 2 Spurs 1. (Fenwick [pen])

Another defeat and the same old story. We shouldn't have been beaten and yet we lost! We can't keep saying that, even if it is true.

We created so many chances against their back four who didn't have enough pace to cope with Paul Stewart. We kept putting Paul in but nothing came of our dominance. Then, out of the blue, they scored and it was one of those goals when you know that nothing is going your way. A corner came into our area and hit me and bounced into the net. I couldn't believe it and wonder how long things like this can happen.

We got back into the game with a penalty, made for us by Gazza, and I scored. We must get a point, surely, but no. Villa score again and the dressing-room is turned into a morgue.

Dressing-rooms after a defeat are not places you enjoy. Dressing-rooms after our recent run are not places you ever want to be part of. I could tell by the expressions on my teammates that we were all asking ourselves the same questions. How well have we got to play to win? When is the luck going to change? This surely can't be happening to us? But it is and it is up to us to end the rot.

At least we hadn't just bashed the ball forward in desperation. I can think of a lot of teams who would be reverting to basic methods but that is not Terry's style. If you lose your beliefs you might as well pack up.

Wednesday, 1 November. Spurs 0 Blackburn 0

I can't imagine the spirit getting any lower than this. We didn't create anything in this game – a Littlewoods Cup third round tie – and, without question, it is our worst performance of the season. Blackburn are not a bad side but there can be no excuse and in a home Littlewoods Cup tie we should be good enough to beat them. Yes, I am worried about the future now and I can't look back on anything in this game that pleased me.

We have had worse results but it is the way we played that is depressing. In the other matches we have played well and lost through our own stupidity. Tonight we played badly and scrambled a goal-less draw. It is an embarrassing result and a poor performance. The papers will be full of our troubles again tomorrow and who can blame them?

One of the low points of the season. Derby beat us at White Hart Lane and how Ted McMinn scored, squeezing the ball in from such an angle, I will never know. Bobby Mimms got a rollicking in the dressing room for this.

I beat Dean Saunders to the ball in our home defeat by Derby, but he still scored later in the game.

The only good thing to emerge is that we didn't concede a goal. It is a crumb of comfort.

Terry has not cancelled our day off as a punishment, he is not that type of manager. But even he must be running out of patience and we are letting him down badly. He is also taking the brunt of the stick from the press and we should be taking our share with him.

To make matters worse I was booked again and that makes four cautions this season – this game, away at Newcastle, Liverpool and at home to Southampton. I don't think my disciplinary record is bad and I do worry about the inconsistency of referees. I also worry about the reputation that has been given me by some people. Before the home Cup tie with Notts County recently the referee actually pulled me up before the kick-off and warned me. 'I know all about you, Fenwick,' he said. 'Just watch it tonight.' You just have to treat that kind of thing with the contempt it deserves and get on with the game.

Saturday, 5 November. Spurs 1 Derby 3. (Stewart)

The crisis is serious now. We are throwing goals away and losing matches with alarming regularity. Spurs, on the bottom of the First Division, are in trouble.

It is no good hiding facts. On paper we are a good team, out on the pitch we are making mistakes and playing as if we haven't been coached. The fans are asking, 'What the hell is going on?' They have every right to demand answers. The only thing I can say is that we will get it right.

Paul Stewart scored his first goal today and until the last minutes of the first half we looked certain to win at last. We played some good football and only Peter Shilton kept Derby in it with some fine saves.

Then just before half-time we let them equalise with the kind of goal that you wouldn't see in a parks match. It started with Mitchell Thomas and a missed header out on our left flank and it was a mistake that allowed Derby striker Ted McMinn into a dangerous position. I went across to cover and forced McMinn into a position that spelt no danger to us. He had to cross rather than shoot, and when he drove the ball towards our near post I thought to myself 'There is no danger there.' I just couldn't believe it when the ball went in. Bobby seemed to fall over backwards and the ball, struck from the narrowest of angles, went into the net off the inside of his leg. Had he stayed on his feet it was impossible for McMinn to score. It was a terrible blow just before half-time and had exactly the effect on us that I feared as I sat in the dressing-room.

I was furious about the goal and gave Bobby a rollicking on the pitch, an incident picked up by the television cameras.

We didn't play badly in the second half but then conceded two more diabolical goals. For the first Bobby and Gary Mabbutt got in a tangle and Dean Saunders was left to score and then McMinn, again from a narrow angle, shot under Bobby's body. Had he stayed on his feet again McMinn couldn't possibly have found the net!

It is becoming a sick joke. We are playing well and against Derby outfought them and outplayed them for much of the game, and yet we lose. What is going wrong? No one seems to have the answer.

The tension among us finally cracked after the game. Gazza had a go at Bobby and a lot of inner frustration boiled over. Gazza struck a nerve and a fracas developed. There were no punches thrown but they had to be pulled apart and quietened down.

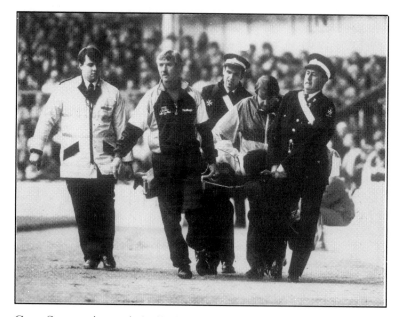

Gary Stevens is carried off after the terrible tackle by Vinny Jones. It was a controversial incident and put Gary out of the game for the rest of the season.

It is half-time against Wimbledon and it looks as though the referee and I have a lot to consider. We have, Gary Stevens had just been carried off after the Vinny Jones tackle.

It seemed to jolt us all into a gloomy situation and we were sitting silently around the dressing-room when Terry came in. He stared hard at Bobby because they had been two bad goals and Bobby is under pressure now. The crowd are getting at him and he is having to live with constant speculation in the papers about his future.

Terry goes on about elementary mistakes. 'Why do this, why do that when we practice all week?' he says and we just nod and agree.

Sunday, 6 November.

I watched Arsenal thrash Forest 4-1 away in the live game on the box and I wasn't that impressed. If these are supposed to be two of the top teams in the country there is hope for us.

The infamous Vinny Jones. His reputation goes before him and he must try and handle the publicity he receives.

It cheered me up after a depressing Saturday night because I feel we have still got a chance to climb right up the table. It is funny but although I haven't been at Spurs long I have developed a real anti-Arsenal feeling. I don't want them to win anything!

Monday, 7 November.

Paul Stewart has said in the papers today that there can be no more excuses. We play Blackburn away in our Littlewoods Cup replay on Wednesday and the game can't come quickly enough.

We have been angered by some comments from their centre-half, Colin Hendry, who has said what Blackburn

92

are going to do to us at Ewood Park. We will see, and, surprisingly, there is a real determination to put the record straight. I think Blackburn are in for a shock.

Wednesday, 9 November. Blackburn 1 Spurs 2 (after extra time). (Thomas, Stewart)

Even the hotel staff at our Blackburn headquarters are giving us stick and the jokes in the national press continue. It is, in fact, getting beyond a joke and we need to put a few people in their place to stop all this nonsense.

We meant business – I could sense it before the game – and we started like a house on fire. We flew into tackles, we knew that pride was at stake and Blackburn didn't like it. Gazza didn't help them with his non-stop banter at their players and a bit of feeling started to creep into the game.

We played well and should have punished Blackburn long before the game went into extra time. Chris Waddle missed a great chance at the far post, hitting the post with a crashing shot when he could, and should, haved just placed it. I thought, 'Oh no, not again', as the chances went begging.

Then Mitchell put us ahead in extra time and the relief flooded out of the players. It was as if this was the goal and the result we had been waiting for. And we were playing so well at the back that I just couldn't see them scoring. But then, catastrophe. We gave away another diabolical goal.

Poor Guy Butters, making his debut, after coming on as a substitute, is credited with an own goal and yet it was hardly his fault. Bobby came for a cross, stopped and shouted, 'Away'. But Butters was already committed and his header sailed up and into the top of the net. It was a tragedy for the youngster who had done really well and showed maturity beyond his years.

93

I went berserk at Mimms. We hadn't given them a chance and yet, here we were again, in danger of throwing things away. I screamed at Bobby – why didn't he come out and clatter everyone in clearing the ball? Mistakes happen to everyone but they are occurring too regularly for our liking.

We were rescued by Paul Stewart and a goal that showed exactly why the boss paid a reported £1.7 million for him. His power and determination took him past three Blackburn defenders and Paul finished the run with a neat cross shot into the net. It was a great goal and how we needed it. Gazza couldn't hide his happiness and took delight in baiting the Blackburn defenders. He had had a running battle with them all night and, thankfully, had won.

You would have thought we had won the League when the final whistle went. It was the happiest we have been all season and Hendry, the Blackburn player who slagged us off in the press, was standing in the tunnel as we trooped off. He had been suspended for this game and yet, boy, did he take some stick!

It was a great journey home and time to reflect on a victory. Only a little one but a very important night for Spurs. Could this be the turning-point?

Friday, 11 November.

A normal training session for a Friday but we play Wimbledon tomorrow and a lot of time is spent on practising set pieces, especially those against us. Wimbledon are a strong, physical side who throw the ball at you from all angles.

I don't believe that Wimbledon enjoy playing against the sweeper system and I am looking forward to the game. Queen's Park Rangers always did well against a side that most teams hate playing. Big Fash is a danger but he is not that mobile and if you keep tight on him half his strengths are wiped out. He will be looking for flick-ons to get little Terry Gibson in.

Saturday, 12 November. Spurs 3 Wimbledon 2. (Fenwick [pen], Butters, Samways)

We outfought Wimbledon, out-Wimbledoned them, out-manoeuvred them in midfield and should have scored more goals. This scoreline flatters the Dons. We played well and now it is two wins on the trot!

The game was marred by an incident that was the talking-point after the game, and sure to dominate the papers over the next few days. Vinny Jones went in for an unnecessary tackle on Gary Stevens who was carried off. His knee injury looks serious.

It appears to me as if Jones is trying to live up to his image. He isn't that tough, certainly doesn't go round whacking people, and yet is clearly starting to believe the label given to him by the media. There was no need for him to get involved with Stevens as Gary and Fashanu tangled for the ball out on the touchline. He could have pulled the ball out and got on with the game but he chose to dive in and he caught Gary's knee. But the linesman, standing right by the incident, didn't flag for a foul, the referee didn't give a free kick and I have to say I thought it was a foolish tackle. Just completely unnecessary.

I really believe that Vinny has got a problem with his own image. He seems to want to live up to it.

The incident must have hurt and affected him because he pulled out of every challenge after that. He just didn't want to know and the Stevens injury seemed to destroy him.

Gary has been taken to hospital and the feeling is that he could be out for some time with damaged knee ligaments. It is a terrible blow for him because he was just battling back after a series of injury setbacks.

His injury, and the Jones inquest, mustn't hide the fact that this is an important win for us.

Wednesday, 16 November.

This is a free week for us although Chris and Gazza are away with England in Saudi Arabia. As expected, the Jones incident is dominating the papers. The other issue is that everyone is expecting Paul to get his full debut for England.

Bobby Robson, however, only names him as substitute and plays Michael Thomas of Arsenal instead. I can't really understand that, and why take Alan Smith and Brian Marwood of Arsenal and only use them as subs I just don't know.

I went to school with Brian and he always had great skill but was shy and reserved. He is certainly not a physical player but is a great crosser of the ball from either flank. He was brought on towards the end of the 1-1 draw and, again, why take a 29-year-old to a friendly in Saudi and only give him a few minutes? The same goes for Alan Smith. Why not play them both from the start, just to see what they can do? It is certainly impossible to make an impact in the last ten minutes or so.

It was a poor performance and a disappointing one. We should be thrashing teams like Saudi Arabia and I can remember playing in a 4-0 victory in Egypt and being surprised when the England team got slaughtered by the press. This time I sat at home and thought to myself, 'I am glad I'm not involved with this one.'

Michael Thomas looked as though he had found the step up from the club to international football extremely hard.

Saturday, 19 November.

Tomorrow is our first 'live' showing on television, away to Sheffield Wednesday. It is an important game for us because we feel we have something to prove to the nation. We want to show that we are not as bad as our results. There is certainly a new mood of confidence as we travel up to Sheffield after a short training session.

Sunday, 20 November. Sheffield Wednesday 0 Spurs 2. (Stewart 2)

It has been snowing in the North and we are disappointed that Wednesday have not made more of an effort to get the pitch cleared. When kitman Ray Reyland went down to Hillsborough to lay out our shirts at lunchtime the goal areas and centre circles were cleared and yet nothing else was done. It is not worth worrying about, however, and our attitude is to just get on with the game.

We played well, knocked the ball about, looked tight at the back and proved a point to a lot of people. There was a first-half incident that became the talking-point of the game although for me it was just a storm in a teacup. Paul Stewart chased a ball into the area and collided with their goalkeeper Chris Turner. Wednesday made a meal of it and the referee spoke to Paul but I am sure it was a case of TV making it look worse than it was. Like the Paul Davis incident, people get carried away just because they see it on television. You keep hearing managers say that they would love a big centre-forward who gets stuck in. We have got one and he is getting criticised.

Paul, however, had the last laugh with two second-half goals and he really is growing in confidence now. One was a great individual effort, the other was a little fortunate with Turner rushing out and then, I thought, stopping slightly.

He probably thought he was going to get clobbered again by Paul.

At least the nation has seen that we are not a bunch of mugs.

Monday, 21 November.

We are being linked with a string of goalkeepers as the pressure mounts on Bobby Mimms. The irony is that we have won our last three games but keepers like David Seaman of Queen's Park Rangers are said to be top of our list. We have four at the club, Bobby, two sixteen-year-olds and £100,000 Peter Guthrie, who hasn't had any first-team experience yet. One name I keep hearing is that of a Norwegian international called Erik Thorstvedt and I know that Ray Clemence, our goalkeeper coach and scout, rates him highly. I do think we need another experienced goalkeeper on the staff, if only for competition.

Wednesday, 23 November. Spurs 1 Coventry 1. (Stewart)

I don't know how many times this has happened this season but the one thing I do know, it is getting ridiculous. We played well yet didn't win. We had Coventry by the throat and let them escape and in the end they went close to winning.

After the victories over Sheffield Wednesday, Wimbledon and Blackburn it is particularly disappointing. We proved a point to the nation and our fans at Hillsborough on Sunday and slipped back again tonight. We all thought that the win at Hillsborough was going to be the turning-point of the season and yet we have clearly got a lot of work still to do.

Paul Stewart scored again, putting us ahead, and I am pleased for him because he was very down at the start of the season when he was suspended and then couldn't find his touch in front of goal when he eventually came into the side. It can only be good for us if he has started to score because, although we have given away crazy goals, we haven't been scoring enough either.

Friday, 25 November.

Spurs are looking at Thorstvedt, the Norwegian goalkeeper, and he was at the training ground today. The pressure is right on Bobby now.

It is ironic that Bobby seems to have come through his worst patch and is playing well again. That often happens in football. You are under the microscope, the club signs someone else and then you start to play to your full potential. If Bobby continues to set a higher standard it is going to be a difficult selection problem for the manager.

Erik Thorstvedt only trained with the reserves and the first-team players have yet to be introduced, which is usually the responsibility of the captain. The club are still waiting for full clearance for Erik before officially signing him and that should be in a couple of weeks.

Saturday, 26 November. Spurs 2 Queen's Park Rangers 2. (Gascoigne, Waddle)

After 20 minutes I couldn't believe what was happening. Rangers were 2-0 ahead and we were in disarray. I felt the whole season had dropped right back to square one. And it had to be against my old club!

Both goals were fortunate, although we shouldn't be relying on excuses at this stage of the season. A ricochet enabled Mark Falco to strike a goal that, as soon as he hit it, was always going in. It was just one of those strikes that comes your way once or twice a season. Then we got in a tangle at the far post and Falco played it back across for Trevor Francis to make it two.

At that stage we were in a mess and struggling to hold on. It wasn't the first time I had played against my old teammates. At the end of last season we played at The Bush and lost, but this felt worse.

We were thrown a lifeline by Chris Waddle, who scored with a header just before half-time and that made the dressing-room a slightly happier place. Instead of being on the floor we took some hope from Waddle's goal. It was a good time to score.

Dressing-rooms at half-time are places for the manager and his players. Allan Harris usually stands guard at the door while Terry goes through what we are doing wrong. He is good and usually picks up things that have not been obvious to players. The goal this time has helped us and there is a definite feeling of being able to get back into the game.

The days of a cup of tea at half-time are gone. It is now soft drinks, juices and energy drinks, and I usually sip an orange juice and sit down and stretch out my legs. There is no ritual, the players just relax quietly while the manager has his say. We get 15 minutes together and the time zips by as if it was seconds.

It is no surprise when we equalise and it is another Gazza special. He is so quick at taking free kicks in dangerous positions and, not for the first time, the goalkeeper doesn't move as the ball flies in. David Seaman is very experienced and yet the Rangers were caught out. They must have known that Paul's speciality is free kicks from the edge of the box.

Like in so many other matches, it is a Jekyll and Hyde performance. We have just not hit any consistency. We came close to winning the game and that, after being 2-0 down, is a good performance on paper. But I am not particularly happy. We haven't learned enough as a team for my liking and have not developed as a unit with the season. It is difficult to put my finger on why we are so inconsistent.

The dressing-room is a happier place, more out of relief. A few players on the fringe of the team come in and offer advice and thoughts and the players discuss another performance. It is, however, another two dropped points.

Monday, 28 November.

We play Southampton away tomorrow in one of our most important matches of the season. It is the Littlewoods Cup fourth round and we just can't afford to lose. Our inconsistency in the League means we have no chance of challenging for the Championship, I realise that now. That means we must make an impression in the cups if we are to keep our season alive.

We train and leave for Southampton by coach about two-thirty. It is only a couple of hours by coach and it is a good idea to travel early and stay overnight because there is nothing worse than rushing at the last minute after being delayed by traffic or a breakdown. We made that mistake at Charlton in October and were fined by the Football League after arriving late and failing to give in the teamsheet at the latest time allowed by the League.

That was due to a nightmare route taken by our coach driver who decided that the quickest way to Charlton from our Royal Lancaster Hotel headquarters was via Earls Court, Stamford Bridge, Wandsworth and Streatham. I know that part of London well and after about five miles I knew that something was wrong and that he was going the 'long way round'. I shouted from the back of the coach and tried to make him change his mind, but he had the route planned in his mind, and we were late. It is the coach company who take the responsibility for getting us to the games on time and they have to pay the fine if they fail to meet the deadlines. I don't know what got into the driver's mind but his company coughed up the League's £200 penalty.

Tuesday, 29 November. Southampton 2 Spurs 1 (Own goal).

One of the low points of the season. We are out of the Littlewoods Cup, a competition I thought we had a great chance of doing well in. There was a mood of 'We must do well' before the kick-off but once again we blew it. We missed chances and lost a game when we were the better side. It is the story of our season and a very worrying situation.

It was typical of our luck that Southampton took the lead with a long 30-yard pot-shot from Glenn Cockerill that hit my shoulder, changed direction and flew into the opposite corner. It was a miserable goal to concede.

The ridiculous thing is that we had not been threatened and yet found ourselves a goal down. How many times have I said that already this season? We had a penalty appeal turned down and created and missed chances where they scored again in the second half. When is our luck going to change?

It did for a split second when Russell Osman put through his own goal to haul us back into the game and we then dominated the game for long periods. There was a great chance for Gazza after he had been set up by Chris Waddle. But he snatched at the opening and it proved to be our last hope on a night when, once again, everything went wrong.

It is difficult to gauge exactly what is happening to our season. We are not a bad side and yet, at the moment, we are heading nowhere. Adrift in the First Division, out of one major Cup competition and struggling to hit any real consistency. Why aren't we doing it? It is a question we keep asking ourselves and something I turn over in my mind all the time.

The dressing-room after the game is a quiet, depressed place and Terry, who is usually bright and full of ideas after matches, just says we missed too many chances and walks out. There is no hiding-place now for the club, we are all in this together.

It is a long, silent journey home. At the start of the season I honestly believed that Spurs were good enough to win something big. Maybe we are going to have to wait for the team to bed down with Terry's ideas for a little longer. Maybe next season. Who knows? I mull over all this on the way back to London and it is a recurring nightmare.

Wednesday, 30 November.

At last some good news. The Football League have restored the two points they deducted from us for the 'game that never was' against Coventry on the opening day of the season.

The players knew there was an appeal but deep down none of us expected the decision to be reversed. The chairman and Terry always believed that the original punishment was a joke and went to Lancaster Gate for the appeal full of confidence. I thought it would be a sign of weakness on the League's part, however, and was staggered when the news came through. The decision has lifted the club, pushed us away from the clutches of relegation and helped wipe away the memory of last night. Perhaps our luck is changing, at last.

EARNING MY SPURS

Friday, 2 December.

The press are still giving us a great deal of criticism and yet I feel that deep down they appreciate what we are trying to achieve. They can see we are trying to play the right kind of football and it would be great for the game in this country if Spurs could get it right, especially with players like Chris and Gazza in full flow.

Saturday, 3 December. Everton 1 Spurs 0.

Another typical result. We play well and lose. I am sorry but it is true. I have never been to Goodison Park and totally outplayed Everton but that is what happened today. I can't believe the result and yet it is there in black and white.

We got a slap in the face in the opening minutes when Tony Cottee scored a goal that was so offside it was embarrassing. Television proved that it should never have been allowed and I admit that a feeling of 'Oh no, not again' went through my mind. I wonder what Spurs have done to deserve such injustice.

We continue to defend well and miss chances and this really has been the hallmark of our season. Gazza looked sharp and after one great run through the Everton defence his shot was cleared off the line by Stuart McColl with Neville Southall beaten.

I have known Terry Venables a long time and I can see he is getting uptight about the fact we are losing matches after playing so well. We are not quite hitting it off and it is difficult for him to understand.

In the dressing-room he tried to be positive and yet there are signs that frustration is creeping up on him. He had been very positive before the game because he was pleased with the League's decision to restore the two points to our total. He had been determined that Spurs would win the case even though the decision came so quickly. Tottenham, I understand, were prepared to go to the High Court to win. Deep down I wonder how determined he is in his belief that 'this' Spurs side can give him what he wants.

This game was my first look of the season at Tony Cottee, at a reported £2.5 million the costliest player in Britain behind Ian Rush. Arsenal were also chasing Cottee before the start of the season and in the end he decided to leave West Ham for Everton. I have always enjoyed playing against Cottee because as long as you can keep him in front of you and deny him space you have got a chance. It is only when you are level and in a race that you find yourself struggling against his pace. He is never going to beat you for skill and relies on his poaching around the box. Today

Fen, John Gregory and Gary Lineker, who was destined to join Spurs.

he struggled and looked ordinary. He got the goal and can count himself extremely lucky.

Monday, 5 December.

We are moving towards the end of 1988 in a sea of frustration. I hope this is not going to turn out as the season that 'almost happened' for Spurs.

This week there is the Football League six-a-side tournament at the G-Mex Centre Building in Manchester and we have decided not to send any first-team players. Terry believes that we are under enough pressure not to expose ourselves to more media activity. I can just imagine the headlines if we played and went out to a smaller club. Spurs instead send a reserve side and there is talk of a fine from the League but the decision was made in the best interest of the players and club.

He gives us two days off this week to take our minds away from the worries of battling to make things come right.

It is the normal pattern under Terry to step up the training just before Christmas and then let it die right down into the New Year. He has always felt that players need a boost of fitness to get them through the second half of the season.

Saturday, 10 December. Spurs 2 Millwall 0. (Waddle, Gascoigne)

Millwall are one of the surprise sides of the season. Manager John Docherty has moulded them into a team who are holding their own with all the big boys and it is refreshing this season that so many of the unfancied clubs are challenging at the top. Millwall, Coventry, Southampton and Norwich are all producing results that no one expected.

Millwall play a long game, aiming most of their attacks at twin strikers Tony Cascarino and Teddy Sheringham. Today they just played into our hands and the sweeper system is tailor-made to deal with these kind of tactics. I don't think they created one clear-cut chance and on the day we totally outclassed them.

The sweeper system is a game that I believe suits our side because it allows players like Chris Waddle and Gazza more room and time to express their superb talents. It also allows the opposition more space, however, and, deep down, I wonder if Terry will change back to a flat back four this this season? Teams like Everton and Arsenal condense the game, we intend to stretch it out.

Chris Waddle scored a great goal in the first half and Gazza struck another of his free kick specials from outside the area to kill the game off. I don't know why goalkeepers haven't sussed Gazza yet. Millwall's Brian Horne went behind the defensive wall to try and line it up properly and the ball was in the net in a flash. We always have a player in the wall doing the lining up so our goalkeeper can keep his eye on the ball all the time.

There is no question in my mind that this is close to our best performance of the season. I thought we played well at Everton but this is definitely one of our best results. Millwall came to White Hart Lane flying and we took advantage of their tactics and produced a really professional performance. The atmosphere in the dressing-room is good but I am not getting carried away. I have thought about turning-points all season and we have stumbled so often. Ask me again in a month!

This is a free week and I am not bothered either way about having days off or playing matches. All the fuss about too much football certainly didn't come from the players them-selves and had they been asked when the chairmen decided to lobby for a cutback in the First Division the professionals would certainly have answered: We prefer to play in games. The reductions that have been made make no difference to stamina, preparation or tactics and I am certain that the fans would always want football to watch. If their team is successful the supporters will go to the games, regardless of how many times a week, or the cost.

We work hard in training this week under Terry's policy of get tough in the middle of the season. We don't work for more than an hour and a half but it is excessive and the training is with and without the ball.

There are no house rules under Venables. He is not a manager to tell you to stay in on a Friday night or ban sex after Thursday. He leaves it up to you. He treats you like an adult and expects you to respond. Terry was a player and knows what you can and can't get away with, and would soon give you a tug if you were letting yourself or the club down. It is not worth abusing the system. If you don't take care of yourself off the pitch you can't expect to play to the best of your ability and the outcome is that your career suffers.

Saturday, 17 December. West Ham 0 Spurs 2. (Mabbutt, Thomas)

This was Gazza's day. It only lasted 45 minutes for him before he was injured but it was his finest performance of the season so far. He ran the show in the first half and completely dominated the match. He ran it, controlled it and mesmerised West Ham with his magnificent attacking skills.

It was a display that made him look the best player in the country and Terry must have been proud sitting in the dugout. What a pity it lasted only half the game. He got a whack across the ankle from Paul Ince and it was obvious at half-time that he could take no further part in the game. I hope the ankle injury is not going to keep him out for long because there are signs now that things are coming together and we certainly need Gazza in this kind of form.

He can do everything on days like this. He tackled, passed, won balls in the air, got in great attacking positions and was doing his work at the back. Some players have rich qualities while Paul has the lot. His will to win is also first-class and behind his public mask of happy-go-lucky is a serious side and a strong ambition. If everything can be harnessed in the right direction we have got one hell of a player in this country.

West Ham were typical today. They buzz for about 20 minutes and then drop their heads and their workrate when things don't happen. I have seen it so many times. Gary Mabbutt scored in the first half and Mitchell Thomas won the points with a delightful chipped goal.

We haven't conceded a goal for two matches now and things are looking good. I was pleased that we overcame the disappointment of losing Gazza to maintain our standard in the second half.

The draw for the FA Cup third round was made tonight and we have been paired away to Second Division Bradford. It is not an easy tie, although I fancy us to get through. We are in the right mood to deal with them and I don't have any fears of a Cup defeat.

Monday, 19 December.

It is Christmas week and an extremely difficult time for footballers, especially married men with families. Somehow you have to try and balance out the problem of club commitments with spending time with your wife and children, although it is almost impossible. Terry tries to give

Christmas is a difficult time for players and their families. This is my son George.

us as much time off as possible but so often we are caught in the middle.

We are weighed twice a week at Spurs and this is not the best time of year for watching the pounds. Friends pop in at home, the kids are excited, and I admit that I often find it difficult to concentrate 100 per cent on football at Christmas.

110

Wednesday, 21 December.

The Spurs players have been under a lot of pressure this season. So much was expected of us, it went wrong and we have paid for it in criticism and disappointment. So today we had a 'get away from it all' Christmas party in London. It was just the players. All 18 members of the regular first-team squad went on a happy-go-lucky pub crawl and it was a great success. There was a theme to the party of silly hats and bow ties and you can guess who wore the biggest and the silliest. Gazza came as JR and kept up his act the whole night! We started in mid-afternoon and crawled into our beds in the early hours, a bit the worse for wear but relaxed, and I was happy that the lads had been together to get things off their chests.

Thursday, 22 December.

We were supposed to have today off to recover but the boss has called us in. I wonder why? He knew we were going out on the town and now we are paying for it.

Terry worked us hard today and we quickly lost all the booze we took on board last night. We trained in the ball court at White Hart Lane. It was stuffy and hot and we went flat out for an hour and a half.

Sunday, 25 December.

Christmas Day and a 'working' day for professional footballers. After spending the majority of the day at home we trained at White Hart Lane at six o'clock in preparation for tomorrow's home match with Luton, and then checked into the West Lodge Park Hotel on the outskirts of London:

It sounds tough on families but players have to be right in body and mind and, after all, it is our livelihood at stake. The other thing to consider is that a footballer's career doesn't go on for years and, although we are well-paid, it can end quickly and without warning.

For instance, I have just bought a small hotel in Durham. I am a great believer in looking after the pennies and investing wisely. My wife Amanda and children George, six, and Nicholas, four, have a good lifestyle and we have learned to cope with the strange hours and pressure of working on all public holidays.

Monday, 26 December. Spurs 0 Luton 0.

A desperate game and a bitterly disappointing result for us after our recent performance. The scoreline is a joke and we should have walked away with the points.

I missed a penalty today – my first miss for Spurs – and it is a bad thing. I had scored against Luton goalkeeper Les Sealey last season when I put the ball to his left and I should have stayed with my favourite side. But as I walked up to take the kick I changed my mind, he guessed right and I didn't put enough pace on the ball to beat him. Your heart sinks when you see the goalkeeper save, or the ball go wide, and yet there is nothing you can do about it. Your attitude must be to pick yourself up, put the miss out of your mind and just get on with the game. The next one, however, will be a difficult one.

The fact remains that we should never have had to rely on my penalty to win the game. We missed chances before it and our finishing got worse after Sealey's save. We should have netted five at least.

Gazza tried a comeback but his ankle isn't right. He had a test early in the morning, made the decision in the dressing-room, only to take another whack on it and pull out of the match. He went home for Boxing Day lunch but the only good thing to emerge from a poor match was that we have not conceded a goal for three games.

Friday, 30 December.

Terry has had a public go at Wimbledon's style of play in one of the national papers, and if I am honest I have to say that I don't agree with 'big' names in the game criticising and attacking teams and individuals. These days there is money to be made from such articles and it has become an accepted part of football to 'knock' each other.

I don't believe it is healthy or does the game any good. You should be able to express an opinion but too much of it is done just for the sake of cash. I am not saying that this was Terry's motivation although I am surprised that he went public. I know his feelings about Wimbledon's long ball and physical game, and yet I would like to see him encouraging and helping. He has got so much to offer the game, and too much to lose.

I try to avoid it and sometimes cringe when people like Emlyn Hughes and Mick Channon, two old professionals who earned so much from the game, continually rubbish it. I can't believe that they need the money that badly.

I am not a great admirer of Vinny Jones, and yet I think he takes too much stick from people now outside the game. I enjoyed it when the Wimbledon 'hard man' decided to have a go back at Ian St John and Jimmy Greaves who had criticised him on their Saturday television programme. Jones looked up St John's record and discovered that the

How this wasn't a penalty we will never know. Chris Waddle is brought down by Arsenal's John Lukic but the referee said play on. It was a joke decision.

Saint had been sent off more times than him, even being dismissed in friendlies. I liked that, it was a question of a player standing up for himself against the onslaught of criticism that some people seem to enjoy dumping on football.

Saturday, 1 December. Spurs 2 Newcastle 0. (Walsh, Waddle)

Jim Smith has taken over at Newcastle and one of the big clubs in the country are starting a revival and making a bid for First Division safety. Smith has signed Kenny Sansom from Arsenal, bought Kevin Brock from his old club Queen's Park Rangers, and his enthusiasm for the game has rubbed off on the players and supporters. So this was another pleasing result for us, especially the clean sheet. It wasn't a great game and yet it was the kind of performance that allows you to think that Spurs, at last, are putting their bad season behind them.

It was particularly pleasing for Paul Walsh, who scored only his second goal of the season and first since 1 October. When an individual is going through a tough time it is not usually discussed in the dressing-room, and it is more likely to come out in the get-togethers the players have started to have in the coffee bar close to the training ground. Paul's goal certainly made his agent Eric Hall a happy man. Eric had £100 at 9-1 in the club betting shop that Paul would score the first goal of the game!

Walshy got his goal early in the match, and although Newcastle improved in the second half we were always in control. I heard that afterwards Smith said that his team missed enough chances to have won, but I never felt that we were stretched at the back. Chris Waddle's goal only arrived at the perfect time to kill them off.

Michael Thomas of Arsenal, a vital part of the Arsenal machine, holds me off at White Hart Lane.

A sight that no Spurs fan likes to see, an Arsenal goal. It's the winner at Highbury.

There is another busy schedule ahead. We are allowed home tonight to spend New Year's Eve with our families but tomorrow we are back in training late in the day and then off to our overnight headquarters in preparation for one of the big games of the season, away to Arsenal.

Monday, 2 January. Arsenal 2 Spurs 0.

We are really up for this game. We never seem to get any luck against Arsenal and I feel that this is going to be our revenge. Arsenal for me are too geared up for defending, they let themselves down going forward and I don't think they are so effective at Highbury. We are on an unbeaten run of four games and not giving away any more silly points.

The only disappointment, especially for the Spurs fans, is that Gazza has still not recovered from his ankle injury. He would have loved this stage, a big local derby, more than 45,000 people inside Highbury and an odd kick-off, five-thirty for the live television cameras.

Arsenal scored just as I thought we were holding them and organising ourselves nicely. A ball down the left was played in by Alan Smith and Chris Fairclough seemed to be caught in two minds. Paul Merson ran across him and shot back into Bobby's opposite corner. It was a bad goal for us to concede and not many people realised that the ball bobbled just before Bobby's dive. I felt a bit sorry for him because he had been under pressure with Erik in the background and had responded with some clean sheets.

The turning-point of the game came just before half-time when Chris went through only to be brought down by Arsenal goalkeeper John Lukic. It was an obvious penalty. The crowd seemed to go quiet in expectation of the decision and the only two people who didn't think it was a spot kick were the referee, Alan Seville, and his linesman. I couldn't

117

believe it and can only assume that both men, who were only standing 20 yards away from the incident, bottled it in front of the TV cameras.

To make matters worse, television play-back evidence showed conclusively that it was a penalty. Lukic admitted that he fouled Chris and Arsenal manager George Graham agreed that it was a bad decision. Thanks, ref.

You can ask the referee why he made the wrong decision, and yet what does it achieve? He isn't going to change his mind and all you are doing is releasing your own frustration. What often happens in these situations, however, is that the referee tries to make it up to you in small ways. Sure enough, in the second half he gave us some dodgy free kicks on the edge of their area, decisions that we would not have complained about had they gone the other way. It was almost as if Seville was saying sorry!

We couldn't harp on the penalty too much in our dressing-room discussion at half-time. It had gone. Far more encouraging was the way we had played, and the talk was of getting back into the game. We were still confident of doing it.

We played some of our best football of the season in the second half and completely dominated the game. We should have scored but again missed chances. Chris was guilty of one miss and Paul Stewart, with a few minutes to go, shot straight at Lukic when it seemed he must score.

It would be easy to use the penalty as the only excuse and I know that would sound like sour grapes. The fact that it was a clear penalty just rubbed salt into our wounds.

Even in defeat we were encouraged by our performance. I believe that had the penalty been given we would have gone on to win the game. It is vital that we don't let this result worry us and that we use our second-half performance, and recent results, as our platform for Saturday's FA Cup third round tie at Bradford. If we are going to win anything this season, the Cup-tie is our last chance. It is a vital game for the club and the team Terry Venables has started to build. We certainly can't afford to lose.

Saturday, 7 January. Bradford 1 Spurs 0.

It is difficult to describe my true feelings. As a professional footballer you are conditioned to disappointments, almost ready for setbacks. To be injured, dropped and criticised are all part of a footballer's life, while winning gives you the biggest buzz of all.

Defeats like this eat into you like a bad dream. There is no real beginning or end to a game like this. They just happen.

When I look back on my career I will remember this game as one of the low points. Bradford had knocked Everton out of the Littlewoods Cup and were going well in the Second Division but after the season we have had, this was a game we simply needed to win. I expect the Tottenham critics were sharpening their knives as the minutes ticked away.

The mood in the dressing-room was good. The Arsenal defeat was out of our system and we were relaxed in the knowledge that we had played well at Highbury in front of the television cameras. The TV boys were here again, no doubt just waiting for the upset.

We started well enough and Mabbs almost scored in the opening minutes with a header. It was a chance he would normally take, especially as he is so good in the air.

The goal that knocked us out was an elementary mistake by Mitchell Thomas, although it would be unfair to blame one player for us going out of the FA Cup in the third round. The fact, though, is that Mitchell left his place to join the defensive wall for a Bradford free kick before anyone had covered him. It was not a quick free kick but as soon as their skipper Mick Kennedy saw the space he pushed the ball into the gap and full-back Brian Mitchell came thundering up to score with a low shot. The golden rule is, never leave your position unless you are covered. Mitchell did and we were punished. It was a goal that also took a wicked bounce just as Bobby went down to save it.

Mitchell held up his hands in the dressing-room at half-time and apologised for his error. Half-time discussions are not the time for inquests. The game is alive and it needs more positive talk. Terry says what has happened has gone and there is nothing that we can do about that now. He firmly believes that we can get at least a replay out of the game and we are all confident of pulling it round.

The longer the tie went on the worse it became for us. We dominated long periods and were the better side. We just didn't create any chances and by the time the last 15 minutes approached we had lost our shape and ideas. We were panicking as a team, taking the easy way out by pumping long balls forward, using route one instead of playing it short. Another golden Tottenham rule broken. Terry has always stressed: never panic, be patient, play your football. He hates the long ball game and yet here we were playing it.

When you are going out of the Cup it is a horrible thing. We were rushing the game as a side and if there were messages being shouted from the bench, I didn't hear them. Bradford knew they were outplayed, and they also knew they were getting away with it. This was not humiliating like last season at Port Vale, although it was bad enough.

The final whistle. The cold realisation that you are out. Swear words enter your head, you shake a few hands and trudge off. The fans chant your name and you wonder why. Fans – they really are amazing the way they stick with their club and I feel so sorry for them. It is a long way to Bradford and their journey home is going to be a long and, yes, bitter one.

The dressing-room is like a morgue, not for the first time this season. Terry is strutting up and down. He can't believe how we played, he can't believe the result. It is fact, how-ever, and the news that non-League Sutton have knocked out First Division Coventry doesn't really soften our blow.

There is plenty of time to reflect on the way home. Not much is said, no one really feels like eating, and the first thing you want to do after a result like this is play again. Who have we got next week? Forest at home on the box. Another live game, more exposure.

The Sunday papers will no doubt have a go at us. They will be laughing again. It is a cruel game and yet we must stand up and be counted. It is no good feeling sorry for ourselves. We must prove we are big enough to take it and bounce back. There is no reason why we should not string some League results together and surprise a few people by finishing in the top six in the First Division!

Monday, 9 January.

The inquest.

Terry is disgusted with the team and who can blame him? He doesn't just point a finger at Mitchell over the goal but blames the entire side. He says it was an unprofessional goal to give away and stresses that the whole team had gone to sleep.

This is one of the real low points of the season. The entire squad is locked together in the dressing-room before train-ing to explain away what has gone wrong. And it isn't just the defeat at Bradford that is tossed over in conversation, the last six months come under scrutiny. On paper Spurs should be one of the top sides in the country, and yet here we are, in the wrong half of the First Division and now out of both cup competitions. We have just got to find some answers before the end of the season.

Gary, Chris and I, the three senior members of the side, have more to say than most because perhaps we feel it the

The nightmare of live television, and this is Erik Thorstvedt's worst moment of his career. It is his debut against Nottingham Forest at White Hart lane and, whoops, the ball goes in through his fingers. He recovered, however, to play superbly for the rest of the season.

hardest. Young players have everything before them – senior professionals know that every season is precious, offering up the chance to win the prizes that every footballer dreams of.

Gazza didn't play at Bradford and it is interesting to hear his thoughts. The game from the stand is a different situation, and at least we have got the defeat out of our system.

Terry spends a lot of time strutting up and down. One great quality about him is that he never slags us off in public, only if we really deserve it. He kept his cool immediately after the game even though it obviously hurt him. He made it clear that he never wants to see a side of his thump the ball long again. Whatever the circumstances, he says, keep playing, let it come, rather than give it the big slog.

We expected a bad press and they have had a field day. Coventry have been knocked out by non-League Sutton and yet those reports are of Sutton's joys. Ours are all linked with Spurs' new desperation.

By the time we finished training the Bradford nightmare has been forgotten. We have wiped the slate clean.

Thursday, 12 January.

Bobby is axed from the side and discovers before training today. There has been so much speculation about Spurs and their goalkeepers that I am sure no one outside the club is really surprised. My own feeling is that with big Erik in the background Terry had to make a decision before long. Bobby almost got it right but it wasn't perfect at the back, we know that.

Bobby is bitterly disappointed. He has played in all 26 League and Cup games this season and must feel that he has been made a scapegoat for the defeat at Bradford. We all held our hands up and admitted that we played badly, but Terry is the manager and is paid to make big decisions. Bobby's is the head that has gone.

It is difficult for the players because we can't compare Bobby to Erik. Apart from a few looks at him in training he is just another face to us. Had it been David Seaman of Queen's Park Rangers (Terry admits that he made a £1 million cash bid for him) coming into the side, it would be easier for us to pass judgement. We don't know what Erik is like. Does he stay on his line, come out, shout, cover? No one knows.

He joined in full training this morning for the first time and certainly looks good. He is confident, has good reflexes and seems to command his box. It is so different in a match, however. Just ask Bobby!

Saturday, 14 January.

We play Forest at home tomorrow in front of the live TV cameras. You have to try and treat these television games as just another match although there is a different buzz about the place with cameras outside the dressing-rooms and watching your every move. A lot of people don't like the intrusion of the cameras and yet I don't see how football can complain after taking £44 million from ITV. It also gives the public an insight into the game. No, I wouldn't dismiss it at all and I'm certain televised football is here to stay.

Sunday, 15 January. Spurs 1 Nottingham Forest 2. (Waddle)

Poor Erik had a nightmare.

We started badly as a team and Forest, with their skill and one-touch football, knocked us out of our stride. They were still terrible goals to concede. The first from Gary Parker skimmed past Erik and squeezed inside the post and then he made a mess of a pot-shot from Nigel Clough and let it slip out of his hands and over the line.

How could you feel anything but sympathy for him? No one means to make such mistakes, especially on your debut, at home, and in front of television cameras. My own thoughts at the time were a mixture of 'Oh no, not again' and 'When is our luck going to change?' We switch the goalkeeper and it still happens to us!

For the two days Erik had trained with the first team he looked so commanding and confident, I would have bet money on him keeping a clean sheet. At half-time in the dressing-room he tried to put on a brave face and said that nothing like that had ever happened to him before. We had to try and forget it because Chris had headed us back into the game just before the interval and the last thing we needed was another defeat following the Bradford setback.

We dominated the second half without really looking dangerous or threatening to open Forest up. It is a bitter disappointment and I really am getting fed up with saying that this season.

Forest are a good side, they counter-attack so well and Brian Clough certainly manages to squeeze the very last drop of talent out of his players. Take Parker – his career has been resurrected. I have a lot of time for Clough's sides although I am not a lover of how he handles himself away from his players.

Erik is alone with his disappointment after the game and it is difficult to know what to do for him. Poor fella – new teammates, new game, new club and this happens. I think it will take him a few weeks to get over it.

Tuesday, 17 January. Spurs 1 Monaco 3. (Moncur [pen])

We just didn't need this friendly following the setbacks against Bradford and Forest. I didn't play after collecting a slight knock on the knee against Forest. Had it been a

League game I would have carried on but I was happy to drop out.

Monaco were on fire and wiped the floor with us in the first 20 minutes. Mark Hateley played, although the disappointment for the fans was that Glenn Hoddle has picked up an injury and stayed behind in France for treatment. There is talk of a cartilage operation!

Friday, 20 January.

I like going back to my native north-east to see my family and friends although I find it hard playing in front of so many people I know. It adds to the pressure, especially after our recent results and the season we have had. I still have to find 20 tickets for family and friends for the game at 'Boro tomorrow!

Saturday, 21 January. Middlesbrough 2 Spurs 2. (Stewart 2)

This was Chris Waddle's game and how we didn't win it I don't know. I know I have said this so many times and yet it is true. The Middlesbrough supporters actually applauded us off the pitch at half-time because the quality of our football was so high.

How they took the lead and then equalised with ten minutes left after Paul Stewart's two goals I will never know. We should have killed them off. We had so much pressure, dominated the game and played some superb football and in the end had just one point to show for it.

Chris was outstanding and he certainly deserves to win something this season. Perhaps he will get the Footballer of the Year vote even at the end of a disappointing season with

Spurs. He is the type of player who must be encouraged and the way he is playing this season he should be a regular for England. It always amazes me that we have players of rich talent like this and don't use them properly at international level.

I would have Gazza and Chris playing together for England now. You have got to give Chris the ball, allow him freedom, and why he isn't playing up front for his country is a joke. He has been England's best forward all season.

He has never been outstanding for England and you have to begin to think it is the way he is used by Bobby Robson and Don Howe. Chris tore the Middlesbrough defence apart and how exciting it would be to see him cutting up foreign opposition like this.

Chris, Gazza, Paul Walsh and I stopped up in the North-East after the game. I have bought a small hotel in Durham and it allowed me to take care of a little business. We all drove back on Sunday afternoon.

Wednesday, 25 January.

Gazza has signed a boot contract with a company called Brooks that, they say, will make him a millionaire off the pitch. Good luck to him and I don't begrudge any professional footballer money. He has got his whole career in front of him and as long as he realises that without results on the pitch he is dead, he will be OK.

I think he tried to live up to his reputation in the opening couple of weeks of the season before settling down. He was unlucky to be injured just when he was bombing and playing his best football for us, but he is fit again now and desperate to produce the goods once more. He is an amazing bloke and nothing seems to worry him. He treats life as a bit of fun and his favourite comment after today's deal is, 'I'm Gazza, and I'm loaded.'

EARNING MY SPURS

Saturday, 28 January.

It is FA Cup fourth round day and one of the worst Saturdays of the season if you are already out of the Cup. We were going to play Portsmouth in a friendly but it is too wet after days of torrential rain.

Tuesday, 31 January.

Gazza has had a blow-up at the Toy Fair exhibition in London. It seems to have been mishandled by his agent and Paul got angry about being pressed to dress up in a DJ Bear suit. It seems no one could agree on whether any payments were being made for the personal appearance and the whole thing got out of hand. You don't often see Gazza angry and he must have been upset to let it get out of control.

Saturday, 4 February.

Paul Stewart got some 'stick' today after we travelled to Manchester for tomorrow's live TV game against United at Old Trafford. He was recognised by some of the hotel staff and Paul discovered exactly what they thought of his move to London from City and his current form!

If we are away the night before a game we usually go to the cinema, and most of the players went to see the film *Cocktail* tonight. Even if it is a film you don't particularly want to see, it passes the time and that's important.

Sunday, 5 February. Manchester United 1 Spurs 0.

This is a poor game for the cameras and a disappointing one to play in. You can't really explain why some matches don't jump into life, while others are on the boil from the first

minute. This was one I bet the London Weekend organis-
ers wish they hadn't chosen. Long before the end the crowd
were getting impatient.

Even the goal that decided the points was messy. Gordon
Strachan's cross from the right went through my legs and
Brian McClair slipped it into the net. Poor Erik, two of his
first three games have been on television and we have lost
them both.

I was booked in this game after a tackle on Mark Hughes.
I thought it was a fair challenge, one of those when both
players go for the ball and it is six of one and half a dozen
of the other. Paul Stewart was also booked and we are now
both automatically suspended for two matches. The club
keep a record of all individual cautions and I knew that I
was facing a suspension when I went into the game. How
can you let that stop you tackling or challenging? You just
have to get on with your normal game.

The club has a strict disciplinary code, and any player
booked for dissent loses 25 per cent of his weekly wage. You
are not fined for a tackle and the frustration is that your
suspension and fine is in the hands of inconsistent referees.
One week a player can be cautioned for a silly comment, the
next you see a terrible tackle go unpunished.

Terry feels strongly about the on-field discipline and he is
always going on to Paul and Gazza about being booked for
silly, niggly things. Bookings and suspensions are no good
to football clubs if they are challenging for the top honours,
or even trying to stay clear of relegation.

At the moment we are caught in no-man's-land, right in
the middle of a mediocre season. It is up to the players to
show what we are made of and to make an effort to climb
the table and finish as high as possible. The top six has got
to be our target. With the three-point system that goal is not
out of our reach. We may be in 13th position but our attitude
has got to be to give it a crack and prove to our critics that
Spurs, at least, are still alive and kicking.

Wednesday, 8 February.

Chris pulled out of the England squad after the United game while Gazza flew out on Monday with the rest of the team, and we are all rooting for him. It is only a friendly and it is the ideal opportunity to make a couple of changes and experiment. What has the England manager got to lose?

Gazza was only a sub, alas, and got just a few minutes at the end of the game. What a waste, and surely if a player is worth £2 million and is rated the most skilful player in the country, he is worth a look at in a meaningless friendly? It is such a waste of talent and an opportunity gone to give a player like Paul valuable international experience.

England beat Greece 2-1 thanks to Bryan Robson, although it looked a poor game.

Thursday, 9 February.

I got confirmation today from the Football Association that I am suspended for two matches and it's only what I expected. There is nothing I can do about it except sit out the matches and kick my heels.

The boss and Gazza have also been told that they could face a charge of bringing the game into disrepute for comments made in the media. Terry is in trouble for his anti-Wimbledon remarks and Paul got involved in a slanging match with his old Newcastle directors. They are entitled to their opinions but I don't think anyone can complain when the FA, who are trying to clean up the game, react.

Terry and Paul are two of the biggest names in soccer and they should understand that what they say makes instant headlines. It also only heaps more pressure on the club midway through a season that has been hard enough, and

I don't have any real sympathy for them. It is their own fault.

Saturday, 11 February. Spurs 1 Charlton 1. (Stewart)

I am booked again! There was a 50-50 ball and their midfield player Andy Peake and I both went for it. I thought I got the ball first, only for the referee to blow up and say that I followed through. I asked him what the problem was and said that I went for, and got, the ball but he wasn't a referee to discuss the situation with you. You learn how to judge officials and he was one to leave alone. He had made a decision and was sticking with it but I was still disappointed with the booking.

Terry is very strict about getting booked for dissent. He is always going on about on-field behaviour and I agree with him, though referees are so inconsistent. You can argue with one, discuss a situation with another, while others get the book out at the slightest comment.

When you look at the match programme before a game and see who the official is, the worst thing you can do is say in the dressing-room that this fella is a good one. He turns out to be a disaster. The referees still come into the players' room before a game to discuss their own rules, and some are quick and interesting while others drone on for about ten minutes. The players normally end up looking at each other and whispering, 'What have we got here?' I just wish all referees would control the game as they see it, let it flow and not stop the action for every little thing.

We should be able to beat sides like Charlton. At the start of the season when you look at the fixtures this is a game that should be a home banker for a club like Spurs. It was however the same old story. We had the chances, missed them and they broke away through Paul Williams to score. It was a bad goal to concede, they caught us napping and Erik was also disappointed to let it through. Paul Stewart grabbed us a point with an equaliser but we obtained no real pleasure from the result or performance.

Monday, 13 February.

We were fined £200 by the League today for arriving late at Charlton back in October. The bill has gone straight to the coach company.

It is a free week with no game on Saturday. There is plenty of time to digest the season again and I would prefer to be playing. At a club like Spurs it seems strange not to be involved when the season is heading towards an exciting climax for those clubs involved in all the prizes. If we don't adopt that attitude the rest of the season will dissolve into one long anticlimax.

It is a depressing prospect for me at the moment. We don't have a game until next Tuesday against Norwich and even then I must start my two-match suspension. It is going to be a long wait.

Tuesday, 21 February. Spurs 2 Norwich 1. (Gascoigne, Waddle)

Terry had to make changes because Paul Stewart and I are both suspended. Nayim, a lovely little player from Barcelona who is on loan at White Hart Lane, makes his debut and Paul Walsh comes back into the side as the boss shuffles his pack. Terry reverts from the sweeper system in defence to a flat back four.

When you are suspended you normally drop out of the first-team squad and train with the reserves. After every session Paul and I also trained on our own to keep the fitness level up although 'Stewy' pulled a hamstring and spent most of his first-team isolation in the treatment room. It is hard work being suspended and the club train their first-team players hard. It is also hard watching and I hate sitting in the stand knowing that I should be involved in the action.

Norwich are going well and are still the surprise package of the season. They are right up there with Arsenal at the top. Liverpool are also looking dangerous and you can't rule them out of the Championship race.

We played well and Gazza got a great goal after a through ball from Nayim. I worry about foreign players coming into the First Division and whether they can cope with the physical side of the game. Nayim, however, looks as though he will be able to cope.

Norwich are an impressive side and I like the way they play their football. It was no real surprise when they equalised and the most encouraging part of our performance tonight is that we came back to win it. It showed that we are not on the floor, despite our results, and still have the character to prove a few critics wrong.

Chris Waddle won us the game with a shot that he smashed past Bryan Gunn. I say it was a bit of a fluke although Chris, surprise, surprise, doesn't agree with me.

Saturday, 25 February. Southampton 0 Spurs 2. (Waddle, Nayim)

Gazza is also suspended today and this result is a great boost for the club and a tribute to the young players who have filled in, like Nayim and Mark Robson. Mitchell Thomas has also been recalled in the last couple of matches and has done a good job.

You like to see the team do well, of course, although it does make you worry when you are sitting at home and waiting for the results to flick up on Teletext. The inevitable reaction is 'Will I get back in?'

I didn't travel with the team today and when I saw the weather I knew I had made the right decision. It is filthy and the Southampton pitch is turned into a quagmire. Gazza and I trained on our own at White Hart Lane before shooting off to hear the results and I was delighted when I'd heard that Nayim had got the second goal from a free kick. Chris got the first with a superb chip and he really is playing well.

We are now unbeaten in three matches, have won our last two and if only we can keep this going. I know it is late but maybe this is the turning-point.

Monday, 27 February.

I am back in training with the first-team squad, which is a big relief after the last two results, and so is Paul Stewart. But who drops out of the side to play against Aston Villa on Wednesday night?

Terry has a quiet word with me and says that he wants to keep a flat back four and that I will be playing centre midfield against Villa. It is good to be back in the side although I would prefer to be in defence. The answer to the team selection is that Mitchell, who has filled in well for the last two games, drops out but the boss doesn't recall Paul and he has to be satisfied with a seat on the subs bench.

Wednesday, 1 March. Spurs 2 Aston Villa 0. (Waddle 2)

This was another special performance from Chris and if any awards this season are based on entertainment he should be Player of the Year. He scored two and should have got a hat-trick; both goals were superb efforts and typical Chris – running at defenders, beating them and then lashing in the ball. When he plays like this there isn't a more exciting forward in the country.

The England players meet up tomorrow for the World Cup tie in Albania next week and I don't see how Bobby Robson can ignore Chris in this form. He is really enjoying his free role and I would play him down the middle with Gary Lineker.

Friday, 3 March.

There are no First Division matches tomorrow because of the England World Cup tie but we are in training because we play a friendly with Bordeaux at White Hart Lane. It keeps us ticking over, I suppose, although I am not a great believer in specially arranged matches that mean nothing.

With Chris and Gazza on international duty Terry can experiment with his team and I am playing left-back tomorrow. It is a little disappointing for me because I like more involvement and it is obvious now that Terry has no intention of switching back to the defensive sweeper system.

Saturday, 4 March. Spurs 1 Bordeaux 2. (Mabbutt)

A game against the French side clearly didn't mean much to the Spurs fans either, not even with the added attraction of Clive Allen's first return to White Hart Lane. The tiny crowd that bothered to turn up is the smallest in the history of the club. Terry didn't even bother to watch either and went instead on a scouting mission to Fulham.

It was a poor game without any atmosphere and Clive will be delighted that he scored. He produced a typical performance, one we saw at Spurs so often. Clive is either very good or very ordinary.

Wednesday, 8 March.

England win 2-0 in Albania and it is a victory that Bobby Robson and the country needed so badly. The performance, alas, was disappointing again.

The biggest frustration for me, watching from my arm-chair, was the display again of Chris. He just can't do it for England and I know he will be gutted at not turning it on, especially after being selected in his favourite free role down the middle. I just don't understand why Chris doesn't stamp his authority on the England scene. I can't remember when he was not outstanding for us and yet he is a different player with England. It can't be inexperience, he doesn't suffer from nerves, he has pace, great ball skills and is an intelligent footballer. Yet, like so many players before him, it doesn't happen for him on the international stage.

Gary Lineker is not the same player he was before his hepatitis illness, although Robson is not going to leave out his premier marksman. So the pressure is on Chris and I just hope he is given another chance in that role. It will come good for him in the end, I am sure of that. I have my doubts, however, about the pairing of them as an international front double act.

Saturday, 11 March. Derby 1 Spurs 1. (Gascoigne)

Another position. I am at right-back this time and that is three different shirts I have worn since my suspension. It just shows you what happens when you are out of the side.

This time Chris Fairclough is the man to drop out and Paul Stewart is recalled up front in a reshuffled side. Gazza is also back. Derby are tough opposition and their defensive record is superb and it is a solid, professional performance from us that earns a point. We were even disappointed with their goal. Dean Saunders did well to score and yet Gary and Guy were kicking themselves after letting him escape and get through.

When you have a player like Gascoigne in your side there is always a chance that he will muster something out of nothing and this was a typical example. A free kick on the edge of the box didn't look particularly dangerous because the angle was acute but somehow he squeezed it past Peter Shilton.

While Gazza went off on his war dance I couldn't help thinking that the Shilton of old would have stopped this shot. I firmly believe that Shilts was frightened of getting injured and colliding with the post, he just flapped at it and didn't even dive. A few years ago Peter would have dived and tipped it round the post without even thinking of the post or getting injured.

Let's get it right, Shilts is still a hell of a 'keeper. But is he as good as he was? At 39 years old there have to be question marks and he definitely doesn't like coming off his line so much. At his age who can blame him? Would you want to come out for a 50-50 ball with someone like John Fashanu? He is probably not even aware, although subconsciously he is doing things differently.

I am 29 and I would like to think I could carry on playing until I was 35 or 36, especially in a sweeper role if Terry ever goes back to that system. Shilts is amazing and it is credit to him that he has looked after himself so well and is still England's number one, and he thoroughly deserves the century of caps he collected earlier this season.

Whisper it quietly, we are unbeaten in our last five League matches!

Monday, 13 March.

We don't play this week and it is a relaxed few days around the club. We are not doing much training and the boss has even given us two days off.

Saturday, 18 March. Coventry 1 Spurs 1. (Waddle)

Chris hasn't mentioned England ever since he returned from Albania and it is not something that is brought up in the dressing-room. If a player is worried about form or a performance he usually gets it out of his system in his own way.

Gazza gets the treatment from Coventry's Lloyd McGrath today. He follows Paul everywhere in the first half and eventually catches his studs across Paul's ankle and forces him out of the game. It is a blow because ever since he sustained his ankle injury at West Ham back in December Gazza hasn't had a long run in the side to enable him to get his form back again. He was brilliant before and during the West Ham game and it must be frustrating for him. He is going to have to live with close markers, however, and the treatment will get worse as his reputation grows. McGrath, having no one to mark in the second half, was eventually pulled out of the action. He had done his job and was suddenly superfluous to Coventry's needs.

We were disappointed with Coventry's goal. It came from a knock-down, and we are beginning to concede too many like this. Once again Chris is our saviour and after he equalised we grew in confidence and could have won the game in the end when we hit a post.

Tuesday, 21 March.

We trained this morning and then travelled up to Nottingham for our game against Forest tomorrow night. Gazza's ankle has not recovered and he is replaced by David Howells, another of the youngsters I know that Terry has a lot of confidence in.

The unbeaten run is now six games and this is the biggest test of our mini-revival. There is a good spirit in the camp and if only we could have strung together some performances like this earlier in the season . . . if only.

Forest have just beaten Arsenal to maintain their Championship challenge. It is interesting at the top of the First Division now. Norwich have been caught, Arsenal are favourites for the title although Liverpool, as always, are never out of it and approaching the leaders like an express train. We are not expected to win this match.

Wednesday, 22 March. Nottingham Forest 1 Spurs 2. (Howells, Samways)

We surprised a lot of people tonight. A lot of the critics who wrote us off at the start of the season will look at this result and admit that, perhaps, they made a mistake.

We played Forest at their own game, we sat off a little bit and denied them space, we broke well and Terry must take a lot of credit for one of the shock results of the season. He put little things in our mind and warned us to get back behind the ball quickly when our attacking options broke down.

I think Forest were surprised at the quality of our passing and there can be no question marks against our character now. We came from behind at Derby and Coventry and Forest took the lead in this match, a silly goal when we were caught sleeping at the start of the second half. The spirit is such that it didn't surprise me when we equalised through David Howells and in the last minute substitute Vinny Samways got the winner.

That's Forest's Championship hopes shattered. They are in two Cup finals already this season, the Littlewoods and Simod, and heading for the FA Cup too. They can forget the League now and I know we could have challenged for the title if we had only got our act together earlier.

We didn't see Brian Clough tonight. He has been banned from the touchline and was sitting up in the grandstand. I bet his team heard him after the game, though!

Thursday, 23 March.

In Nottingham yesterday Chris Fairclough pulled out of the squad when he was told that Leeds manager Howard Wilkinson wanted to talk over a possible £500,000 transfer. I don't think Chris wants to leave Tottenham but he can see his chances are limited, especially with Terry switching to a flat back four and with the emergence this season of young Guy Butters at the heart of the defence.

Today is transfer deadline day when all deals have to be completed by the five o'clock deadline. Leeds are trying to rush the Fairclough transfer through in time but Chris isn't in a hurry and keeps Wilkinson waiting until the last minute. He eventually only signs on loan, just to beat the clock and free himself to play in Leeds' bid for Second Division promotion. I will be sorry to see Chris leave Spurs, he is a lovely lad and his transfer emphasises how strange football can be. One minute you have a teammate, the next you have a rival.

Saturday, 25 March.

Another live game tomorrow and this time it is extremely important. We are unbeaten in seven matches now and need to show the nation that we have recovered totally from our dreadful start to the season. It should be a cracking game because Liverpool are also on a winning streak in their late bid for the Championship.

Gazza still isn't fit, which is a blow because he loves this kind of stage. Not surprisingly, Terry keeps the side that won at Forest.

We train today but only lightly because at this stage of the season players don't need to hammer themselves into the ground. It is just a question of going over a few set pieces.

Sunday, 26 March. Spurs 1 Liverpool 2. (Fenwick [pen])

We are confident of beating them and our plan is to 'sit back' and allow them to panic and not hit us on the break. We are to build up slowly and comfortably rather than push the game to them from the word go. It works well and we are much the better side in the first half. We should have had a penalty when Nayim was brought down and the TV cameras later proved that it was a definite spot-kick. But Nayim probably made a meal of it and rolled over one too many times.

We did get a penalty directly after the start of the second half and this time there was no dispute as Paul Stewart was brought down by Gary Ablett. I had thought about taking a penalty before the game, probably because the cameras were here and the fact that it would be my first one since missing against Luton. You just have to blank those thoughts from your mind as you walk towards the box, pick up the ball and put it on the spot. I made up my mind to go, as normal, to the goalkeeper's left, and hit it well in exactly the spot I wanted. Bruce went the wrong way and it was a good feeling to see the ball go in. I am delighted to get that penalty out of the way.

There is no question that we deserved the lead and now it was important to hold them at bay for as long as possible. If we could keep our composure and shape for 20 minutes we would be in business.

Liverpool's answer was to cut through us like a knife. Our fans had hardly stopped celebrating when they strung together a move. Ray Houghton got into a dangerous position and Paul Allen, who hesitated on the edge of the area for a split second, brought Houghton down. John Aldridge

One of the great players in English football, John Barnes. Here he and I sprint it out.

scored and you could feel the confidence start to pump through the Liverpool players.

They turned it on for about 15 minutes. Erik made a superb save from Houghton, Aldridge had a goal disallowed for something that nobody could work out – for me it was a definite goal – and finally Peter Beardsley put them in front. It was the comeback of champions, if only we could have had time to steady ourselves and yet it was impossible against the wave of attacks.

We did regain some attacking confidence and Paul Stewart had a chance near the end only to choose to cut inside instead of shooting and Liverpool kept us out. It is a disappointing result but I am not too upset because we have played well and proved that we are a much better side than our season suggests.

Liverpool for me are still the best team in the country. Forest play the best football but I always get the impression that they will blow up and fade. Arsenal have the organisation and yet Liverpool seem to mix the flair with organisation and they are going to take some stopping. They are on a winning run at the vital time and seem to have the title in their hands. I always like to have the points in the bag and yet Liverpool have an ominous look about them.

I hope Norwich win it because that takes the pressure away from us. We don't want one of the big clubs to become champions, especially our arch-rivals Arsenal. That would be the worst thing to happen after our season of despair.

I have a lot of time for John Aldridge. Everyone thought he was on his way out when Ian Rush returned from Italy at the start of the season and yet he has shown tremendous character to hang on in there and his 21 goals speak volumes for the kind of player and person he is. I had an interesting chat the other day with Chris Waddle and it seems that Peter Beardsley is the one who worries the most about the shadow of Rush. Peter fears that he will be the only one who drops out and it is significant that Beardsley's best form has come with Rush injured and out of the side.

The turning-point of the game was the goal we gave away so quickly after taking the lead and Terry shows his disappointment in the dressing-room after the game. This was an important day for Tottenham in front of the armchair critics.

Monday, 27 March.

We discussed the Liverpool defeat at length today before training. Terry believes that we let them off the hook and they only really started to play after equalising. We allowed them to knock it about rather than hold them at bay. It sounds sour grapes to say that we were the better side and yet, deep down, it's what we firmly believe. That is an indication of how we have developed in recent weeks.

Tuesday, 28 March. Luton 1 Spurs 3. (Walsh, Howells, Gascoigne)

Luton have dropped right into the relegation area and this is one of the worst Luton sides I have seen. They always used to play football through players like Ricky Hill and yet tonight they just thumped it forward looking for Mick Harford. Relegation has really got to them because the worst thing you can do on a plastic surface is just whack it long.

They did take the lead when Guy didn't get close enough to Steve Foster and yet we were not really worried because we were always in control and threatening to score. Walshy and David Howells put us ahead and then Gazza, back for this game in place of Nayim, got the kind of goal that only special players can score. He has threatened to do it so often, almost produced it out of the hat at Everton and tonight brought the house down by running at the Luton defence, beating two defenders, tricking another and slipping the ball in. The whole thing was done in a flash and Luton looked dumbstruck. They are fighting for their lives and a goal like that is the last thing you want to happen to you.

I was booked again tonight and again it was an example of inconsistent refereeing, although it could have been avoided if Mabbs and Allan Harris had passed on a message from the referee before the game. When they went in to see the referee before kick-off he said that he would not tolerate anyone kicking the ball away, and when I was penalised out on the touchline I just backheeled the ball and he booked me. Had I been told I wouldn't have done it but, more

144

importantly, a lot of referees would not even have considered this a bookable offence.

It is good to bounce back after one defeat and there is a strong feeling of confidence and character running through the game. We are getting good results against good sides and, after doing it the hard way this season, we are definitely earning our Spurs. The atmosphere inside the club is excellent and we could have beaten Luton by four or five goals.

We play West Ham on Saturday and games now hold no fear for us. Unlike the beginning of the season, we are looking forward to the games. Terry gives us Wednesday off and yet there is a feeling of disappointment when he announces this – the lads want to stay together and keep on playing.

Saturday, 1 April. Spurs 3 West Ham 0. (Fenwick [pen], Stewart, Nayim)

Before the match we felt that if we could score the first goal West Ham would fold and that's exactly what happened. They went down like a pack of cards.

The season has now gone complete circle. Before Christmas teams couldn't wait to get amongst us, they knew we were struggling and apprehensive and they felt that we were going to be easy meat. Today, opponents look scared of us and our recent run and good results have dealt a great psychological blow. At the start of the season we didn't show enough resilience but now it seems as if teams are in awe of us and we have got the upper hand before the start. We are a big club doing well and that makes a lot of opposition feel inferior.

West Ham arrived at White Hart Lane desperate for points and they showed a little bit of character for about 20 minutes. But as soon as we scored that first goal, they were finished and it is a good feeling for Spurs. These days there is no fear of throwing silly goals away or dropping points. It is only two defeats in 12 matches now and we have risen to sixth place in the First Division! An incredible achievement.

I know it is easy to say now but it doesn't really surprise me. When we were on the floor at the beginning of the season and getting kicked by all the critics I still fancied us to finish strongly, and my only regret is that we didn't string this together earlier. Even a couple of weeks could have put us right there in the frame.

It just goes to show you what can happen. From a slap in the face the entire season has turned and the fans are right back with us. They don't expect us to slip up and players who were affected by our bad results are now maturing and growing in confidence.

Pride has done it and kept us going. It was so humiliating at the start of the season but the players pulled together as a unit and the boss has to take credit for not making any panic moves or changes in attitude. We have had the last laugh.

A strange feature of our victory over West Ham was that there were seven bookings and yet it wasn't a niggly, nasty game and I can't even remember any of the cautions, that's how bad it was! Another day and the referee would not have booked anyone – that is what I mean by lack of consistency.

We now have a break from playing for 11 days and it is very relaxed at the club. The results have helped, of course, and Terry has tapered the workload off. We are now getting a couple of days off at a time and the training is much lighter, only an hour with a little five-a-side burst at the end of it.

I have noticed that we have looked a yard sharper than most teams in the last few weeks and I am sure it is down to Terry's handling of training. He has toned it right down and we are benefiting from the rest.

Monday, 3 April.

Terry has flown to Spain for some business and there is tremendous speculation that he has gone to Barcelona to sign Gary Lineker. It is just like water off a duck's back to the players, we have been linked with so many names this season and when there has been a signing on the boss has always kept the staff informed. I am taking the Lineker situation with a pinch of salt.

Friday, 7 April.

I am feeling my left knee a little bit in training. It is a sharp pain and the problem needs treatment from John Sheridan before and after the session. There is not much of the season left and I am sure it will be OK after a rest in the summer.

Wednesday, 12 April. Spurs 0 Sheffield Wednesday 0.

Wednesday are desperate for points and we have to hold our hands up, they deserved this draw.

It was a bad game for the fans and must have been so frustrating for them after our recent run – 'relegation' matches are often grim affairs. Wednesday are in trouble and are fighting for their lives under new manager Ron Atkinson. On this showing they will survive the drop into the Second Division. They look to have too much character to go down and that must be credit to Atkinson. They had the outstanding player on the pitch in striker David Hirst. I thought he had a marvellous game and was a constant threat to us.

It is a disappointing result for us because had we won this we were looking at a possible place in the top three or four. We had some chances but I take nothing away from Wednesday.

Saturday, 15 April. Wimbledon 1 Spurs 2. (Waddle, Stewart)

The media are trying to make something of this game that just isn't there. When Wimbledon came to White Hart Lane back in November there was the controversial incident when Vinny Jones put Gary Stevens out of the match with an unnecessary tackle and the suggestions are that there could be bad feeling. It couldn't be further from the truth, however, and we have nothing to prove to Wimbledon. There is no talk of vendettas or anything like that. The spotlight has also been taken away from the game by the two FA Cup semi-finals.

The only thing we proved to Wimbledon is that we are in a different league to them. We slaughtered them and it was a victory for football.

Wimbledon have introduced the tactic of slogging it upfield while we are more purists and it was an extremely satisfying victory. Wimbledon use their method of play extremely well and can intimidate the opposition, but they hold no fears for us in our present mood. We coped with everything they could throw at us. It is a significant result for the new Spurs and everyone did well. It was an outstanding team performance.

We have never been better equipped to deal with Wimbledon. Our recent results have made us mentally tougher and able to cope with situations. The early season doubts have disappeared and the attitude now is – 'OK, let's go, we can beat these . . .' We feel we can win every game and it is good to prove we have lost nothing after the disappointment of the Sheffield Wednesday draw.

I was disappointed with Wimbledon. I am not a lover of how they play and yet their spirit has always been top-class. Today they were never in it and the fight and bite was missing from them.

A key to our recent success has been the growth in confidence of some of the players. Paul Stewart is a prime example and we are beginning to get the best out of him. He had a tough time when he first came into the side and now people are looking at him in a different light, they realise he could be a hell of a player. It is purely a matter of confidence bringing out the best in him.

I am sure that Paul Stewart and Paul Gascoigne, our other big signing at the start of the season, will look back on 1988-89 and think how quickly it has gone. At the start it was a mess and we didn't appear to know what we were doing, today it is almost over and we don't want it to finish. It is difficult coming to a club like Tottenham, especially when the fans are always wanting to compare the current team with the old days. At the start we heard it all the time – 'the old side would have done this, or that' – but now they are only talking about what we are capable of. The talk now is of next season and what we can achieve . . .

Saturday, 15 April, will go down in football history as the Hillsborough disaster, the day 95 Liverpool fans died inside the Sheffield Wednesday ground at a terrible crush six minutes into the start of the semi-final against Nottingham Forest.

The Wimbledon and Spurs players had no idea just how bad the disaster was. We were told there was trouble as we bathed and changed after the match and the speculation kept coming through that people had died. But 95 dead – we just didn't know how bad it was. No one did.

Your first reaction is one of shock. And then, 'Why?' It wasn't until I listened to the news at home on Saturday night that I realised the enormity of the disaster and it left me numb and devastated that such a thing could happen inside my profession.

I normally go out for a couple of drinks on Sunday evenings and my friends were all asking the same questions. How could it happen? And it is impossible to answer them. It leaves you numb and helpless. People assume because you are involved with football you know the answers. But you don't, we are just like everyone else.

My first reaction is that we must make sure that we open our eyes to the faults when they are discovered and update all our stadiums. It is terrible that it takes a tragedy for people in authority to jump into action, but that is a fact of life.

Tuesday, 18 April.

Football is in mourning and the people of Merseyside are in a state of shock. The number of dead has risen to 96. Liverpool have cancelled all their matches for the time being and there is a call from many people to shut down the whole of football.

I have to say here that I can't agree with talk of abandoning the season. My heart goes out to the families who have lost loved ones in the disaster but life must go on. Everyone suffers some kind of tragedy in their lives and you just have to get up and go again.

That sounds cold and callous in black and white but it is how I feel.

It sounds a difficult thing to say, but I do hope that the mourning doesn't go on too long. You can never bring those people back and I don't think we will benefit from allowing emotion to rule decisions taken this week. You just can't call off the FA Cup and forget about a season which has been running for eight months. Life must go on. I come from a mining town and have experienced disasters when members of the family went back to work the next day. It sounds tough but it is true. They had to go back to work.

Friday, 21 April.

The Football League and Football Association haven't handled this week at all well. It seems to me that they are more concerned with whose fault the disaster was rather than what has happened. We have also had the crazy situation of clubs calling matches off without League permission and this week has emphasised that the game has no real leader.

The tragedy has been the topic of conversation from everyone, people in and out of the game, critics who know nothing about the sport and others who care passionately about the game. I watched Wogan on television the other night and the programme was more concerned about how much they had raised than the people who had actually died. It seemed to me it was a matter of prestige to be the biggest fund-raiser.

I just wish the League, FA and other football administrators had sat down together, made decisions, stuck to them and allowed football to move ahead with dignity.

There is a tremendous feeling that the family they call Liverpool have suffered like no one else before. I just wonder how the families and friends of the Bradford disaster victims are feeling at this moment. There was not the call then to end the season, or cancel fixtures! These families have got on with life and I am afraid Liverpool must too.

There is talk of them dropping out of the FA Cup now and I hope they don't. I believe they would regret that decision for a long time.

We are playing Liverpool's neighbours, Everton, tomorrow and the League have now decided that any club can call off a match out of respect to the 96 who have died. Everton, however, had elected to go ahead before that directive and I am sure it is the right decision.

EARNING MY SPURS

Saturday, 22 April. Spurs 2 Everton 1. (Walsh 2)

There is a terrible atmosphere inside White Hart Lane. It is our last home game, the fences have come down and it was due to be a celebration. But the disaster has clearly had its effect and the feeling from the crowd is one of respectful quietness. It is like a reserve training session – you can hear every thump and shout from the players.

I don't believe that any game should have been called off because of the tragedy and yet this was a horrible game to play in, a complete nonentity.

The only player to probably enjoy it today is Paul Walsh, who has struggled all season. Today, however, he got two cracking goals and one of them, a chip from the edge of the area, was a superb effort. It will be ironic if Walshy starts to score now after struggling so long in front of goals. Matches are running out for him.

Monday, 24 April.

There is speculation today that Neville Southall, the Everton goalkeeper, was so upset that he didn't try against us on Saturday. I just can't accept that and I'm certain he tried. At the end of the day we are all professionals earning a living from football and once you start you do your best.

It was certainly a difficult game to play in. The motivation before the start was there but once we kicked off the sting seemed to have been taken out of it. We didn't know whether to get stuck in or treat it like a friendly. But as for not trying, I don't believe it.

My left knee is sore today. I am getting through games only to be left with a numbness in my joint. It disappears again after a couple of hours but it looks as though I am going to need a specialist report. I am fortunate to be playing at right-back because there is no one twisting and turning me like in the centre of defence. Everton, for instance, had no one directly in opposition to me and it was a relief as the pain built up.

I am having daily treatment with John and he is patching me up for training. But it is not the same and you don't move as quickly in training as you do in a game. There are just two matches to go, however, and then I will sort it out. I am sure it is just wear and tear that needs a rest. Looking back on my career, I had seven years on the plastic pitch at Queen's Park Rangers and that is sure to have taken its toll.

Wednesday, 26 April.

England beat Albania 5-0 tonight in a World Cup tie and Spurs can be proud of their contribution. Chris Waddle had one of his best games for England and Gazza came on with about 20 minutes to go and scored a great solo goal. It is about time Paul got his chance, instead of two minutes here and there.

The only snag about Gazza's great entry to the international stage was that he overshadowed Chris, who had played so well. Chris has admitted that he has never really done it for England and I hope this is is breakthrough.

It is about time Gazza started a game, though. He has so much skill and vision and I look around the country and ask myself, 'Who else is there?' The Italians would have had him in a year ago and he would be ready to take on the world now.

Thursday, 27 April.

Bobby Robson, who called Gazza daft as a brush before the England game, has now put him down with some more sarcastic comments. He says that Paul needs two balls and had the ball been kicked into the stand Gazza would have chased it. I am disgusted with that and can't believe that he would put one of his players down like this.

That kind of criticism has got to be kept to the dressing-room and if he feels that about Gazza he should tell Paul himself. Paul may act like a confident happy-go-lucky kid but those Robson comments will have hurt him. I certainly

Paul Stewart and Gazza celebrate a goal against Millwall in the 5-0 win at the Den.

wouldn't have been happy had the comments been about me and I wonder if Robson is just making it easy for himself the next time, when he leaves him out!

It is crazy, isn't it? A player comes on, scores a brilliant goal, produces flashes of skill that we haven't seen from an England player for years and walks off the park to a kick in the teeth – from the manager. It doesn't take too many knocks on the chin to pop the bubble from a player like Gascoigne.

Friday, 28 April.

Bobby Robson has now said that Paul can be the new George Best and you wonder if he actually thinks before he speaks.

The country wants players like Gazza and Chris Waddle in the team. They want them to be let loose and show a bit of style and class for a change. Let's have it straight – Gazza should be in the team.

I haven't missed training yet although my knee needs more and more treatment before and after the session.

Saturday, 29 April. Millwall 0 Spurs 5. (Stewart [3], Walsh, Samways)

My knee collapsed after 15 minutes and I was helped off. There was no real warning, I just looked over my shoulder at a player coming in behind me and as I went to move into my stride it went with a searing pain. I realised straightaway that it was a serious injury and John Sheridan didn't even come on. I just shouted over to them, 'My knee has gone.' John told me at half-time that he thought it was a cartilage and that is what he had been treating me for over the last few weeks.

I decided to watch the game because even after 15 minutes I had an idea that we were going to have a good day. How right I was! We have felt for some time that we would thrash someone and this was the day. We won 5-0 and it could have been eight. The boys were on fire and it was a pleasure to watch them tear Millwall to pieces with magnificent football. Their goalkeeper Brian Horne even had a blinder and we are just disappointed it took this long into the season to hit our best performance.

I stuck a huge ice pack on my knee in the second half and almost forgot about it as the lads turned on the style. Some of our moves were breathtaking. We out-manoeuvred them, out-thought them and looked a yard sharper.

I asked one of their players, Jimmy Carter, what kind of training they were doing and he said that it was still hard work with a lot of running. It seems that Millwall are training twice as hard as Spurs and I believe that is one of the reasons behind our recent success – we are full of energy and brightness, while other teams appear stale and tired.

Without question, this has been our best performance of the season. And it just shows you what a perfectionist Terry is because he has a go at Paul Stewart and Paul Walsh for wasting chances in the second half. They both shot when a square pass would have produced a certain goal. Nevertheless, he is pleased. Millwall have been in the top four all season and this is our best away victory for a long time. The chairman said that to the boss after the game and his football memory is second to none.

Sunday, 30 April.

I popped in to see the club specialist, John Bronett, at his Essex home this morning. He examined me and said there was a problem and to go to the Princess Grace Hospital tomorrow for some X-rays and tests. It will be a blow to miss the last match of the season, especially as it is away to my old club, Queen's Park Rangers. But the way I feel at the moment, I have no chance.

Monday, 1 May.

It is a cartilage and I have been booked into hospital a week today for the operation. That's my season over and I have been told just to pop in to the club for some ice packs to keep the swelling down.

It is a low-key week because the training has now been wound right down to about 40 minutes a day. There is no problem because the side is picking itself. There is no game this Saturday because the Sheffield Wednesday match was pulled forward to enable the work on the White Hart Lane ground to be started. They are also re-turfing the pitch for the second year running. I don't know what the problem is but the surface was not good in our last home matches. It should all be finished for the start of the next season, I certainly hope so after what happened all those weeks ago on 27 August 1988. Hell, that seems a long time ago now.

Monday, 8 May.

I reported at Princess Grace Hospital at three o'clock for my operation and by nine o'clock I was having a cup of tea and a walk down the corridor for a little exercise. Cartilage operations are amazing these days, they call them key-hole surgery and the laser just peeps in and nips out the damaged piece of cartilage. I expected a huge bandage, scars everywhere and a lot of discomfort, but it was as if I hadn't even been under the knife.

Tuesday, 9 May.

I checked out of hospital at nine and decided to walk to Victoria station to get the train home. It took me about an hour and the leg was a little stiff but the walk did me good. After 15 minutes I felt great.

Friday, 12 May.

No one would know I had a cartilage operation on Monday. I have been at the club every day, doing body exercises this week and some weights and I can even jog. It is keeping me in shape, even though the season is over.

Saturday, 1 May. Queen's Park Rangers 1 Spurs 0.

The defeat is a disappointing end to the season and that just about sums up this first full season for me at Tottenham. It has been frustrating because we all expected so much.

We haven't won anything but we finish the season with a smile on our faces. We have shown our critics and our fans that we can do it. We put the pride back into Spurs.

On reflection the season was always going to be hard. New signings, a new manager also in his first full season, new ideas – perhaps we expected too much. Next season all will be more settled and I would expect to win something. A club like Tottenham has to win big prizes and Terry Venables won't want second best. Our successful run at the end of the season only increases the pressure. We have proved we can do it, proved that we are good enough to challenge. The disappointing season is over, there can be no excuses next time.

Terry wants us to be another Liverpool. There will be more big money signings, more ideas and he won't stop until he has got it right. I said at the beginning of this book that Terry Venables is a winner . . . and he and Spurs will get there together.

Friday, 26 May.

Arsenal have won the championship and it hurts me to say it. But who am I to begrudge them their hour of glory after going to Liverpool and winning 2-0? It is an incredible end to the season for our arch-rivals, and we will just have to bring them down a peg or two next time. I must say however, that I was disappointed with Liverpool's performance tonight, it was way below par.

Tuesday, 20 June.

The Gary Lineker rumours during the season were true! We have signed England's premier striker from Barcelona for a reported £1.2 million. It sounds like a bargain to me. I can't wait for the new season with Gazza, Chris Waddle and Gary Lineker in the same team.

Friday, 7 July.

I can't believe it, we have sold Chris Waddle to Marseilles for an incredible £4.25 million! It is a terrible blow to us all to lose such a player, but Spurs had to accept that kind of offer. It is also a fantastic move for Chris, and any professional in the country would have said yes.

CHAPTER FIVE

The Players

Erik Thorstvedt: After making a boob on his first appearance against Nottingham Forest in front of the television cameras, Erik has shown tremendous character. He has proved himself one of the top goalkeepers in the First Division. He was only on the losing side four times last season, three of them on TV, against Forest, at United and at home to Liverpool. We make sure, however, that he is always on the losing side in the five-a-side matches. We always play the 'old' players against the 'young' ones and we regard him as the weak link!

Bobby Mimms is now on the reserves and it wouldn't surprise me if Bobby was on his way soon. He shouldn't take that as a snub – transfers happen all the time in football. I'm sure he can make a big success of a new club.

The full-back situation is interesting at Spurs. I would have thought that Terry has got his eyes on two new full-backs and that will cause an interesting dilemma. He has played Chris Hughton, Mitchell Thomas, Brian Statham and myself in the full-back position and something has got to give if he goes into the transfer market. My guess is that he will buy two, play a flat back four and leave a lot of competition at the centre of defence.

Guy Butters: This young man was one of the finds of last season. He has shown that he has character and heart to make it right to the top. It was a hell of a season to come into the side but he just kept going, producing consistent performances at the heart of the defence when everything was going wrong. We know we have got the flair in the side but all teams need players to dig in and make it hard for the opposition and Guy is ours. When young players come into the first team they often need to be rested after a few matches but Guy has kept going. He has saved Terry a lot of money and was the main reason why Spurs could afford to sell Chris Fairclough on transfer deadline day.

Gary Mabbutt: The skipper had a real consistent season and was an ever present. He has learned how to play the Terry Venables way and got his reward at the end of the season with a place on the England 'B' tour.

Chris Waddle and *Paul Gascoigne*: Two of the most skilful players in football. Chris was my player of the season, not just for Spurs but for the whole of football. If you are talking about entertainment value then there was only one choice. It was a pleasure to play in the same side as him and he is the kind of player that gives you a buzz when you see him on the ball.

He is a big man but very deceptive. Chris has got wonderful control and a burst of speed that can leave defenders struggling without realising what is going on. He is often criticised for not looking as though he cares about what is going on. He can stroll around with the hangdog look of someone who doesn't want to know, then he flares into life and wins you a game with a touch of genius.

It was also great in training just to see him and Gazza pairing their skills. I have known Chris a few years with England and then with Spurs and I have never known him play as well as he did in what proved to be his last season at White Hart Lane. It is difficult to pick out one game because he dominated so many. I can remember two goals he got in one night game against Aston Villa . . . but there were so many exciting moments.

I know critics and fans still doubt him and yet ask the Spurs players and manager Terry Venables, they swear by him.

There was not a lot of enjoyment to take out of last season apart from our good run at the end but Chris Waddle's consistent brilliance was undoubtedly a highlight. It is no wonder Marseille went to £4.25 million to get him. It broke our hearts to see him go and yet Spurs had to sell at that price. I wonder if it will ever be beaten for a British player?

Gazza is the same, and if he and Chris could have stayed together it was going to be a hell of a time for the Spurs fans. I was disappointed Bobby Robson sent Gazza on the England 'B' tour – he should be in the senior side now. Gazza, though, needs to learn to be more consistent.

Paul Stewart had a similar season to Gazza. Neither of them really hit it off. Paul began to look the part as the side grew in confidence at the end of the season and I am sure he will score a lot of goals.

Paul Walsh was disappointed. You have only to look at his goal record to understand why, but he, like so many other players, began to look good at the end of the season.

David Howells: Another find and one tackle changed his whole season. He had a crunching tackle with Luton's Steve Foster and went right through him and grew in stature from that day. Foster was shaken up and David received so much praise for getting stuck in that it changed his attitude. He adds so much to our midfield and gets in the box and scores goals. If he keeps it going he can become one hell of a player.

Terry Fenwick: I enjoyed the start of the season, even when we were struggling. I like playing the sweeper system and Terry only changed things when I was suspended. I returned to the side, though playing out of position in a full-back role. I am sure the boss will stick with a 4-4-2 system because it brought us success at the end of the season and there is going to be some sorting out to do.

All any player wants is to play in a winning side. Professional footballers want to win prizes, that is why I joined Tottenham Hotspur, that is what I intend to do.